CONTENTS

G000136878

3

CONTENTS

THE
VIENNA
A D D R E S S   B O O K

Text:	Angela Simek, Mary-Rose Tatham
Editor:	Andrew Coleman
Layout:	Cristina Silva
Photography:	Jon Davison
Cartography:	Falk-Verlag

2

We have made every effort to ensure the accuracy of the information in this guide, but prices, telephone numbers, addresses and circumstances in general are constantly subject to alteration. We cannot, therefore, take responsibility for factual errors of this kind.

5

6

V ienna is a dream of a city and in many ways a city of dreams. It still hankers after its old empire, even if the Viennese deny any affection for the old monarchy. The unique position of Vienna, at the centre of Europe – the gateway to the East, the beginning of the Balkans – and its long imperial history, which was abruptly cut off in 1918 with the end of the First World War, have left their mark on the city.

It is a city that exudes history more than most. You cannot get away from it, but neither do you want to – the city centre (the First District), with its proliferation of charming squares, elegant palaces, town houses, churches, fountains and statues, is so fascinating. And Vienna's momentous history has had a tremendous influence on most aspects of life in the city, including food and entertainment. If the Congress of Vienna danced its way to the treaties of the division of Europe in 1814-15, the turbulence of the later 19th century was forgotten to the tunes of the Strauss waltzes; the abundance of music of all sorts on offer upholds the old tradition. Today Vienna is still making history, as the headquarters of the United Nations.

7

As a capital, Vienna is unusual in that so much of what is of interest is to be found in the centre. Everything is within easy walking distance, although should anything seem too far there are the inner-city buses to take you round as well. Indeed, it is possible to spend one's whole time simply meandering around the small cobbled streets, enjoying a shopping spree or sampling the entertainment or gastronomic delights whilst taking in the historic flavour.

The Vienna Address Book gives a cross-section of what the city has to offer: its sights, restaurants, entertainment, hotels, shops and so on. Vienna is a city like no other. Having been once, you will no doubt come back again to savour more of its delights. This book will make each visit an exciting new adventure, as you discover more and more of the city: its past, its present and its future.

Because of its situation at the centre of Europe, the area where Vienna now stands has been constantly trampled over by migrating peoples and marching armies. The first people known to have settled in this area are the Celts, who built a walled settlement up on Leopoldsberg, one of the hills above Nußdorf, around 300 BC. Their name for their new home was probably Vêdunia, meaning 'wooded stream', and it is from this that the name 'Vienna' comes. The settlement was at the crossroads of two prehistoric highways: the Amber route, which ran north to south, and the Danube, which meanders from west to east. In such a position the settlement would have been an important market town.

The Danube was also important to the Roman Empire, as a border keeping out the uncivilized Germanic and Slavonic tribes. Military camps at strategic intervals along its banks strengthened the border: Vindobona (the Roman name for Vienna) was one of these camps, and as elsewhere a bustling civilian town grew up around it, in the area where the Hoher Markt now stands. However, the waves of Vandals, Goths and Huns that raged through eastern Europe led Emperor Theodosius to hand Pannonia (as the area was known) over to its fate in 433 AD.

Tradition has it that Attila the Hun lived in Vienna for a time and that it was here that his marriage to Kriemhild took place. This seemingly unimportant union has been significant in both literature (the 12th-century *Lay of the Nibelungs*) and in music (Richard Wagner's dramatization of the epic *Der Ring der Nibelungen*), and to the tourist area in Austria just above Ybbs on the Danube, where a considerable portion of the tale takes place. However, the Huns did not stay long. Other peoples also tried their luck, but it was not until the Babenbergs finally drove the Magyars back at the end of the first millenium that a sort of peace came to the area.

The Babenbergs were named hereditary dukes of Austria by the Holy Roman Emperor in 1156, and shortly after they had taken control of Vienna the building of churches began in the settlement. The medieval town of Vienna was clustered around three churches – Ruprechtskirche, Peterskirche and Maria am Gestade – and was surrounded by a stone city wall with gates at strategic points.

Archduke Heinrich II Jasomirgott (1114-77) set up his court at what is now the Platz am Hof, and this marked the beginning of Vienna's first golden age. It was, however, Heinrich's son, Leopold V, who really set

The 'Hofburg', testimony to the Austrian monarchy, is the perfect setting for several monuments, among them this one of Franz I.

about extending the town. Much of this was made possible by the enormous amount of money paid by the English as ransom for their crusading king, Richard the Lionheart, who, after a tiff with the Austrian Emperor at Acre, was foolish enough to wander homewards through the heart of his territory only to be caught at Erdberg.

The Babenbergs were also important to the economic development of the town. In 1221 they introduced the *Stapelrecht*, whereby foreign merchants passing through the city had to offer their wares to Viennese merchants before being allowed to proceed any further on their journeys. Consequently, Vienna did not have to rely on its own craftsmen and was able to specialize in luxury goods.

The male line of Babenbergs died out in 1246 and the country fell to Ottokar II of Bohemia. Despite Vienna's support for this king, who not only began rebuilding Stephansdom (St Stephen's Cathedral) but also started work on the Hofburg, Ottokar's opposition to the German king, Rudolf of Habsburg, led to animosity between them, which ended in 1278 when Ottokar was killed in battle. The reign of the Habsburgs had begun.

10

The Habsburgs, in particular Emperor Maximilian, were very adept at arranging marriages in such a way as to enhance their empire. This tendency led Matthias Corvinus, the Hungarian king who had occupied Vienna from 1485 to 1490, to say of the country: 'Let others wage war, while you, happy Austria, arrange marriages.' This skill was to carry the Habsburgs far and extend their empire over much of Europe and even to Latin America. Matthias Corvinus's own kingdom in due course fell to the marriage game as Maximilian arranged a match to bring Hungary under Habsburg jurisdiction. However, Hungarian resistance to this led to the first Turkish siege of Vienna in 1529, when the Hungarians joined forces with their former enemies against Austria. The war ended when a German army arrived to break the siege.

The devastation caused by this war is partly responsible for the small number of Renaissance buildings in Vienna, as active building in the Gothic style came to an abrupt end. However, the distinct lack of 16th-century churches is also due to the Reformation, which was beginning to make itself felt. Despite bloody reprisals in the 1520s, the Lutherans had massive support, and by the end of the 16th century nearly four-fifths of the city was Protestant.

Emperor Ferdinand (ruled 1556-64) called in the Jesuits to try to halt the Reformation and convert Vienna back to Catholicism. The Jesuits were skilful and, with political support, the Counter-Reformation was eventually successful. There was soon an upsurge in the building of monasteries (1614-30) in the capital and, indeed, were it not for the Counter-Reformation we might not have the spectacular display of baroque art that we enjoy in Vienna today.

The Thirty Years' War left its traces everywhere, as did the terrible epidemics of plague that wracked city and countryside alike in the second half of the 17th century. And by 1683 the Turks were yet again sweeping through eastern Europe towards Vienna with a massive army of 200,000. If we had been able to stand on the city walls on 14 July of that year, we would have seen not only the smoke from the devastated suburbs and surrounding countryside (burnt by the Austrians to prevent the Turks finding any provisions) but the awe-inspiring sight of 25,000 colourful Turkish tents around the town. As in 1529, however, the Turks were defeated. In the siege of 1683, the Viennese army of only 16,000 men held out throughout the summer until a large joint Bourbon and Polish army arrived on the Kahlenberg on the night of 9 September 1683 and the Turks were forced to retreat; they were eventually driven out of Europe by Prince Eugen of Savoy.

The period after the Turkish siege was a heyday of both secular and ecclesiastical building. Many of Vienna's palaces and churches either date from this period or underwent such tremendous renovation as to become thoroughly baroque then. The aristocracy made use of the land laid waste before the city walls by building magnificent palaces there as well as within the city limits. The opulence of these palaces displayed all the wealth and standing of their occupants.

11

The ostentatious splendour of the baroque palaces and churches was mirrored by the theatrical spectaculars of the 18th century, no less impressive, or expensive, for their day, than Hollywood today. Leopold I, who was Emperor at this time (1658-1705), was one of the most important patrons of baroque art. He was himself a keen musician and competent composer and at his court he organized many festivals and magnificent operatic performances with huge choirs, orchestras and special effects.

Emperor Karl VI, the pretender to the Spanish throne, on his return from Spain introduced strict Spanish formality and piety to the Austrian court. He also tried to outbuild the magnificent palace of El Escorial at Klosterneuburg, but only an eighth of it was ever finished. His daughter, Maria Theresia, was one of the most fascinating people in Austrian history. Despite ruling much of the time from the bedroom – she gave birth to 16 children! – she was a great reformer, introducing, for example, compulsory school education. She passed on her fervour to her heir, Joseph II, who took his reforms even further. He is remembered most for having dissolved many monasteries and parishes, although his aim was actually to improve religious education, rather than to destroy it. The money he gained by the dissolution was channelled into a special fund which financed newly created parishes until 1900! He was no friend of the spectacular processions and funerals of the baroque era and was himself buried in the most simple of coffins. Joseph II modernized the feudal state by encouraging industrialization and banning slavery, and generally improved living conditions for all his subjects. He is also known for opening up parks, such as Prater, to give ordinary people somewhere to spend their free time. Sadly, his rule was relatively short (from 1765 with his mother, from 1780 to 1790 alone). There followed a period of stagnation, after which the reaction to the Napoleonic wars brought on a time of political suppression that led to the widespread inner migration of the Biedermeier period. The revolution of 1848, when the students rebelled, eventually brought about the downfall, not only of the all-powerful chancellor Metternich (who escaped to London hidden in a laundry basket), but also of the Emperor, Ferdinand, who abdicated and lived in retirement in Prague's Hradschin castle until his death in 1875. He was replaced by his 18-year-old nephew, Franz Joseph, who was to reign until the middle of the First World War.

The early period of the reign of Franz Joseph is known as the *Ringstraßenzeit* (Ring-boulevard era). This refers to the demolition of the city walls and the construction of the grandiose boulevard on the glacis, the open space directly in front of them, with its splendid buildings. It was an era of neo-absolutism, politically speaking, but of great progress in other respects. Technology had advanced to the stage where massive projects could be undertaken, such as the regulation of the Danube to prevent frequent and devastating floods and the provision of a superb water supply for the capital from the Schneeberg mountain to the south. To add to this came first gas, then electricity, the horse (and later electric) tramway and further provisions for social welfare.

Franz Joseph I, despite reigning longer than any other monarch in European history (1848-1916), was in many ways an unlucky emperor. He was unexpectedly called to take the role very young and, although his greatest desire was to be an 'emperor of peace', his reign began with civil unrest and ended in the First World War. His personal life was equally tragic. He married Elisabeth of Bavaria ('Sissy'), a love-match, but Austrian court etiquette (and an Austrian mother-in-law) proved too much for her, and both Sissy and the marriage suffered. Their son and heir, Rudolf, who many felt could have helped Austria to progress into the 20th century, committed suicide with his mistress at Mayerling (although some question whether it really was suicide). Sissy herself was murdered in Geneva in 1898. Both were deaths from which the Emperor never really recovered. His daughter persuaded him to give up his close friendship with the actress Katharina Schratt, leaving him with little joy at the turn of the century.

History moved relentlessly on for the Austro-Hungarian monarchy. Crown Prince Franz Ferdinand and his wife were murdered at Sarajevo, signalling the beginning of the First World War, and Emperor Franz

Joseph died at the age of 86 in 1916. The war resulted both in the end of the 650-year reign of the Habsburgs, when the new Emperor, Karl, was forced to relinquish power, and the loss of the Empire. In 1918, the social structure of Austria was in disarray and the state was uncertain as to whether it could survive economically so drastically reduced in size or whether it should become part of Germany. The politicians of the First Republic (1918-38), under the Social Democratic leadership of Karl Renner, decided to make a go of it, and introduced a number of worthy social schemes, earning the city the title 'Red Vienna'. However, the rise in political awareness brought with it the development of paramilitary groups and civil unrest followed. In 1927, a demonstration against an apparently unjust court decision led to more than 90 people being killed, and in 1934 civil war broke out. After that the Social Democrats and Communists were prohibited and the way was virtually clear for the illegal Nazis to begin their march to power.

13

Austro-Fascism, which had been a bone of contention with the Social Democrats, for its clerical leaning as much as for its political ideas, suffered a severe blow when the chancellor, Dollfuß, was murdered by a Nazi putsch in July 1934. It limped along for four more years before Chancellor Schuschnigg was finally forced to accept Nazis into his cabinet, thus paving the way for Nazi domination. Attempts to secure Social Democrat aid and a referendum of the wishes of the Austrian people concerning annexation by Germany were left too late. The Nazis marched into Austria on 12 March 1938. Wishing to save Austrian blood, the army was told not to defend the country and the annexation was complete. Two days later Hitler spoke to jubilant crowds on the Heldenplatz, whilst others were fleeing the country. The Nazis began their reign of terror and those members of the Jewish community who had not been able to emigrate disappeared rapidly into the concentration camps, and 600 political prisoners and priests were murdered by the Nazis in the Wiener Landesgericht (behind the Rathaus). The Austrian army became part of Hitler's forces and thousands lost their lives in the war.

After the war, Austria was divided up into four sections, each controlled by one of the four allies. Vienna itself was also divided into four. The monument on Schwarzenbergplatz recalls the Russian occupation, which led to many hardships in eastern Austria. Occupation ended and Austria's neutrality was declared on 15 May 1955 when the Austrian State Treaty was signed by the allies and Austria in the Marble Room at Belvedere Palace.

Austria today is, like most Western European states, a multiparty democracy, currently a member of the EFTA and, despite its still strong Eastern European connections, which led to an unexpected economic boom after the fall of the Iron Curtain, is trying to join the EC.

One of Vienna's charming characteristics is its wealth of sights, visibly testifying to the two millennia of its existence from Roman times to now. Unlike many Western capitals, it is history that is most prominent in Vienna, not the modern city. Even graveyards and quite ordinary-looking blocks of flats may have a fascinating past. The town's architectural highlights are from the baroque period and the *fin de siècle*, although there are some fine examples of modern architecture too.

ANCIENT AND MEDIEVAL REMAINS

EXCAVATIONS ON MICHAELERPLATZ   **19** N9   U 3 Herrengasse
1, Michaelerplatz. (Open air, visible at all hours).
Ongoing excavations in the centre of this square reveal Roman, medieval and baroque foundations and vaults; visible from all around the Michaelerplatz.

NEIDHART FRESCOES   **19** N9/10   U 1, U 3 Stephansplatz
1, Tuchlauben 19. Tuesday to Friday 10 a.m.–4 p.m., Saturday 2–6 p.m., Sunday 9 a.m.–1 p.m.
Vienna's oldest frescoes were discovered in 1979 during the renovation of the 'Zum Schwarzen Bock' (Black Goat House). Despite the baroque façade, the origins of the building are much older, and the frescoes depicting the seasons after the poem on the same topic by the Viennese court poet Neidhart von Reuental (*c.*1190-*c.*1246), were executed around 1400. These extremely rare examples of secular medieval frescoes are now open to the public.

ROMAN RUINS AM HOF   **19** N10   U 1, U 3 Stephansplatz
1, Am Hof 9; tel. 535 56 06. Saturday, Sunday 11 a.m.–1 p.m.
The Roman ruins here are part of a main street of the legionary camp Vindobona and are among the oldest remains in Vienna. It is from here that the Romans defended their empire from the barbarians to the north and east.

Opulent fountains and monuments punctuate the streets of Vienna.

ROMAN RUINS   U 1, U 3 Stephansplatz
BELOW THE HOHERMARKT   **19** N9/10
*1, Hoher Markt 3; tel. 535 56 06. Daily except Monday 10 a.m.–12.15
p.m. and 1–4.30 p.m.*
These Roman ruins were part of the buildings of the camp served ini-
tially by a legion of cavalry sent from Britain in the 1st century AD. The
camp was set up on the high banks overlooking the Danube on what
is now the Hohermarkt in the centre of the city. The remains of the *praetorium*, where the Emperor Marcus Aurelius is supposed to have stayed
and subsequently died, can still be seen.

VIRGIL-KAPELLE   **19** N9   U 1, U 3 Stephansplatz
*1, Stephansplatz (Underground station); tel. 513 58 42. Daily except
Monday 10 a.m.–12.15 p.m. and 1–4.30 p.m.*
Remains of a subterranean 13th-century chapel in the direct vicinity of
the Stephansdom. Medieval ceramics in show cases.

16

CHURCHES AND OTHER RELIGIOUS BUILDINGS

AUGUSTINERKIRCHE   **19** N9   U 1, U 3 Stephansplatz
*1, Augustinerstraße 3; tel. 533 70 99. Mass on Sunday 9.00, 9.45, 11.00
a.m., 6.30 p.m., Saturday 6.30 p.m.*
Somewhat hidden to one side of the Josefsplatz, St Augustine's is one
of the more austerely beautiful of Vienna's churches. It was built in 1330-
39 in the Gothic style as a long high hall but the tower was not added
until 1652. It was in this church that the marriage of Napoleon and Marie
Louise took place in 1810, as did that of Emperor Franz Joseph and
Elisabeth in 1854.

     The Augustinerkirche has a long tradition of wonderful choral music
and the choir sings high mass each Sunday at 11 a.m. – usually a mass
by Mozart, Haydn or Schubert.

DEUTSCH ORDENS-KIRCHE   **19** N9   U 1, U 3 Stephansplatz
*1, Singerstraße 7; tel. 513 13 72. Mass on Sunday at 9 a.m., 11 a.m.
(Hungarian) and 7 p.m.*
The Order of the Teutonic Knights has had a church here from the beginning of the 13th century. The present building dates from 1326-75.
In the 17th and 18th centuries it was partly rebuilt, and the original Gothic
church restored as far as possible.

     The adjacent House of the Teutonic Knights has held the treasure
of the order since 1807. Its courtyard, with the magnificent tree in the

centre and the Stephansdom towering above, is one of the most impressive in Vienna.

FRANZISKANERKIRCHE 19 N9   U 1, U 3 Stephansplatz
1, Franziskanerplatz; tel. 512 54 78-0. Mass on Sunday 7, 8, 9, 10 and 11 a.m., 7 p.m., Saturday 4.30 p.m.
Although the Franciscans had their first monastery in Vienna as early as 1451, the present church and monastery were built after the Reformation and only finished in 1611 and 1621, respectively, blending late Gothic and Renaissance styles.

HOFBURGKAPELLE 19 N9   U 1, U 3 Stephansplatz
1, Schweizerhof. Tours on Tuesday and Thursday 2.30–3.30 p.m. Mass on Sunday 8 a.m., 10 a.m. and 12 noon, with the Vienna Boys' Choir at 10 a.m. (Tickets must be bought in advance.)
First mentioned in 1296, the Hofburgkapelle (Court Chapel) was enlarged in 1447-9 and redecorated in the baroque era, but then redecorated in Gothic style in 1802. Only 13 of the wooden statues from the 15th-century interior remain.

17

The Vienna Boys' Choir, which sings here each Sunday, was founded in 1498 by Emperor Maximilian to sing at his daily mass.

KAPUZINERGRUFT/KAISERGRUFT 19 N9 U 1, U 3 Stephansplatz
1, Neuer Markt.
For anyone interested in Habsburg history, the Imperial Crypt is a must. It has been the last resting place of the Habsburg family since the Capuchin Church was built in the early 17th century. Franz Joseph was the last ruling emperor to be buried here, and his wife and their unfortunate son, Rudolf, who committed suicide in Mayerling, are also entombed here. The last Austrian empress, Zita, was laid to rest here in 1989.

KARLSKIRCHE 19 N8   U 1, U 2, U 4 Karlsplatz
4, Kreuzherrengasse 1; tel. 65 61 87. Mass on Sunday 8, 9.30 and 11 a.m., 6.30 p.m., Saturday 6 p.m.
Vienna's grandest baroque church was built between 1716 and 1737 following a vow made by Emperor Charles VI during a serious outbreak of the Black Death. The Karlskirche (St Charles Borromeus), with its pseudo-Byzantine façade flanked by striking columns, was designed by Johann Bernhard Fischer von Erlach and finished by his son. The iinterior, designed by the younger Fischer von Erlach, is very ornate and truly beautiful. The skilful design of the church, with its huge cupola (236ft, 72m high), allows light to flood in, and, reflected by the bright-

ness of the walls, this magnificently illuminates the church even on the dullest day.

KIRCHE AM STEINHOF

🚃 47A, 48A Psychiatrisches Krankenhaus

14, Baumgartner Höhe 1; tel. 94 90 60. Guided tours (in German) on Saturday at 3 p.m., groups by arrangement.

The church belonging to the Psychiatric Hospital of the City of Vienna is one of the gems of Viennese *Jugendstil* architecture (see page 38). It was designed by Otto Wagner and built between 1904 and 1907 in the grounds of the asylum. Situated high on a wooded hill overlooking the pavilions of the hospital and the suburbs of west Vienna, it is crowned with a vast copper dome that is visible for miles. The interior is most interesting, combining the functional with the strikingly beautiful.

MARIA AM GESTADE   19 N10   U 1, U 4 Schwedenplatz

18
1, Salvatorgasse 12; tel. 533 95 94. Mass on Sunday 7.30, 8.15 (Czech), 9, 10 a.m. and 7 p.m., Saturday 6.30 p.m.

As the name suggests, St Mary's on the Bank (first documented in 1158) was once situated on the banks of the Danube. The present appearance, with the delightful filigree spire, dates back to *c.*1394–1414. It has recently been renovated and is possibly Vienna's best example of a Gothic church. Today it is the church of the Czech community in Vienna.

MICHAELERKIRCHE   19 N9   U 1, U 3 Stephansplatz

1, Habsburgergasse 12; tel. 533 70 50. Mass on Sunday 8 a.m., 10 a.m., 12 noon and 6 p.m., Saturday 6 p.m.

Officially the parish church of the First District, St Michael's was formerly the Barnabite parish church of the imperial court. Early parts of the church date from the first half of the 13th century, and the chancel and tower base from the 14th, but there was a succession of alterations over the following centuries. The façade and present appearance date from 1792. The church has remarkable catacombs with mummified corpses on view.

MINORITENKIRCHE   18 M9   U 3 Herrengasse

1, Minoritenplatz 2a; tel. 533 41 62. Mass on Sunday 8.30 a.m. and 11 a.m. (Italian).

The present Gothic Church of the Minor Friars was begun before 1339, replacing an older building, and has, despite attempts at a baroque interior, retained its essentially Gothic appearance, particularly obvious in the 14th-century main door. The strangely blunt tower is the result of damage by Turkish artillery during the sieges in the 16th century, and the emergency roof put on then is still in use. Noteworthy inside the church is the reproduction mural of Leonardo da Vinci's famous *Last Supper* and the statue of the *Madonna della Famiglia* opposite the chancel. Today it is the church of the Italian community in Vienna.

MINORITENKONVENT **18** L10   Tram 43, 44 Spitalgasse

8, Alserstraße 17.
The Convent of the Minor Friars has a couple of memorials to the anti-Nazi resistance, a plaque to the resistance group led by Pater Roman Karl Scholz (executed in 1944 in Vienna) and a memorial room to Pater Maximilian Kolbe, who was murdered in Auschwitz in 1941 and canonized by the Catholic church in 1988.

PETERSKIRCHE **19** N9   U 1, U 3 Stephansplatz

1, Petersplatz 6; tel. 533 64 33. Mass on Sunday 9 a.m., 11.15 a.m. and 5 p.m.,weekdays 11 a.m. and 5 p.m.
Crammed into the middle of one of Vienna's smallest squares, St Peter's was designed by Johann Lukas von Hildebrandt. Famous now as a gem of Viennese baroque and for the quality of its music (the choir sings on all holy days), St Peter's has a long history. Vienna's first church was built here in the late 4th century, although the present building dates from 1702. The church was damaged towards the end of the Second World War, but it has since been restored to its former glory.

19

The interior is the masterly work of the imperial designer Matthias Steinl. The large fresco in the dome is one of the most important works of Johann Michael Rottmayr.

SCHOTTENKIRCHE **18** M10   U 3 Herrengasse

1, Freyung 6; tel. 533 76 78-0. Mass on Sunday 7, 8, 9.30 and 11 a.m., 12 noon, 7 p.m., Saturday 6 p.m.
The Irish monks, missionaries in central Europe during the early Middle Ages, were commonly known as Scots in German, and hence the church and Benedictine monastery founded here was called the Church of the Scots. Its present appearance dates mainly from the 18th and 19th centuries. The monastery owns a collection of paintings, accessible through the quiet courtyard of the Schottenkloster.

STEPHANSDOM **19** N9   U 1, U 3 Stephansplatz

1, Stephansplatz 3; tel. 515 52-0. Mass on Sunday 6, 6.45, 7.30, 8.30, 10, 11.15 a.m., 12 noon, 6 and 9 p.m., Saturday 6 p.m. Guided tours daily 10.30 a.m. and 3 p.m. Sundays and holidays 3 p.m. only.
The 'Steffl', as the Viennese affectionately call St Stephen's Cathedral,

stands majestically in the middle of the busy capital. In a city dominated by the baroque, Stephansdom is a breath of fresh air, with its Gothic spire, intricate stone carvings and the great sense of space and height. Building first began under Archduke Heinrich Jasomirgott between 1137 and 1160. However, the oldest remaining parts of the cathedral, the west façade with its lovely Riesentor (Giant Gate), and the Heidentürme (Towers of the Heathens), date from the new building constructed on the original ground plan during the reign of King Ottokar II of Bohemia (1253-78).

Work on the south tower, the 'Steffl' itself, was begun in 1365. It is 448ft (140m) high: the highest tower to be completed in the Middle Ages and the third highest in the world, with a spiral staircase of 343 steps leading to a watchman's lookout, 246ft (75m) above the street. It was completed by Hans von Prachatitz in 1433. The north tower, 199ft (60m), was never completed. A makeshift Renaissance spire was added in 1529.

The north tower now houses the Pummerin, one of the world's largest bells and the pride of all Austria when it booms out to welcome in the New Year, or on major state and religious occasions. It was made in 1711 from cannons won from the Turks after the siege of 1683 and used to ring out from the Steffl. However, the cathedral suffered major damage in 1945 and the Pummerin crashed to the ground and shattered. It was recast using the carefully collected pieces of the original and installed for safety reasons in the lower north tower in 1952.

Inside, take a good look at the intricate stone filigree pulpit, carved in 1514-15 by Arno Pilgram. The *Fenstergucker* (peeper at the window) is Pilgram himself. He also represented himself in two other places further down the church, up on the north wall; see if you can spot them. The ghoulish should visit the catacombs, which contain a mausoleum of bishops, the tomb of Rudolf IV, 56 urns containing the intestines of the Habsburgs and some plague victims too.

SYNAGOGE DER ISRAELITISCHEN KULTUSGEMEINDE   **19** N10   U 1, U 4 Schwedenplatz

1, Seitenstettengasse 2–4.
Part way up the cobbled street with high town houses on either side is the entrance to the synagogue serving the Jewish community of Vienna. It was built in 1825 by Josef Kornhäusel in the courtyard of residential buildings belonging to the Jewish community, thus conforming to a decree by Joseph II that only Catholic churches could face streets directly. (Against this apparently intolerant decree it should be remembered that Joseph II was the emperor who gave both Jews and Protestants freedom of religion within his Empir.). The strange positioning of this synagogue meant that it alone, of all the 94 prayer rooms and synagogues

which the 170,000 strong Jewish community had before the annexation of Austria by Nazi Germany, survived even the atrocities of the *Kristallnacht* on 9 November 1938, when the Nazis rampaged vandalizing and burning as many Jewish places of worship as possible. Under Nazi rule, most of the Jewish community who were unable to flee were murdered or sent to die in concentration camps. Today the Jewish community here numbers only about 8,000, although this is now increasing.

VOTIVKIRCHE **18** M10   U 2 Schottentor
9, Rooseveltplatz 8; tel. 43 11 92. Mass on Sunday at 8, 9, 10 and 11.15 a.m., 7 p.m., Saturday 6 p.m.
The neo-Gothic Votive Church, with its two towers of exquisitely pierced stonemasonry, was built by H. Ferstel in 1856-79. It was commissioned by Archduke Ferdinand Max (later Emperor Maximilian of Mexico) to show gratitude for the failure of an attempt to assassinate the 18-year-old Emperor Franz Joseph in 1853.

21

WOTRUBAKIRCHE – KIRCHE   🚌 60A Kaserngasse
ZUR HEILIGSTEN DREIFALTIGKEIT
23, Maurer Lange-Gasse 137 (Georgenberg); tel. 88 61 47. Mass on Sunday 10 a.m.
Trinity Church was built in 1974-6 according to plans by the Austrian sculptor Fritz Wotruba (1907-75) and is one of the few architectural realizations of his cubist approach. The church, situated on the hilltop and visible from afar, is also a rare example of architecturally noteworthy modern churches in Vienna. One observer has commented that it looks as if a giant child built it with gigantic toy bricks.

PALACES

Although not all the palaces and town houses in the city are baroque, the majority of them are. Those we list below are only the most famous of the many that you will see whilst wandering around the city.

BELVEDERE
Home of Austria's most celebrated military hero, Prince Eugen of Savoy, the baroque Belvedere Palace, with its picturesque setting and magnificent views, is in fact two palaces, Unteres (the Lower) and Oberes (the Upper) Belvedere. The Lower is at the end of carefully laid-out classical gardens, which slope gracefully upwards to the more important Upper Belvedere on the brow of the hill.

UNTERES BELVEDERE **25** O8   Tram 71 Unteres Belvedere
3, Rennweg 6.

It was in the single-storey Lower Belvedere, built in 1714-16 by Johann Lukas von Hildebrandt, that Prince Eugen actually lived. This was also the residence of the ill-fated Archduke Franz Ferdinand, who was assassinated in Sarajevo in 1914, and the composer Anton Bruckner, who lived in the caretaker's apartment for the last few years of his life. Nowadays it houses the Baroque Museum and the Museum Mittelalterlicher Österreichischer Kunst (see page 45).

OBERES BELVEDERE **25** O8   Tram D Schloß Belvedere
3, Prinz-Eugen-Straße 27.

Built in 1721-23, the Upper Belvedere is possibly Johann Lukas von Hildebrandt's greatest architectural success. Its impressive roof was supposedly inspired by the shape of the tent used by the Turkish grand vizir, which was part of the Austrian booty after the siege. It has seldom been used as a residence, but often for official functions, grand galas and festivities. It was here that the spectacular festival marking Marie Antoinette's departure for France to marry Louis XVI was celebrated in 1770. It was here too that Göring enjoyed playing the role of the great Reichsmarschall. A far happier celebration took place on 12 May 1955, when the Austrian State Treaty was signed in the Marble Hall, ending the occupation of Austria by the Allies and declaring Austrian neutrality.

22

Today the Upper Belvedere houses the Österreichische Galerie des 19. und 20. Jahrhunderts (see page 46).

HOFBURG **18** M9   U 3 Herrengasse
1, Hofburg. Guided tours, from the entrance under the dome of the Michaelertrakt, include the opulent apartments in the Reichskanzleitrakt and the Amalienburg.

The Imperial Palace sprawls not only over a considerable area of the city but also over the centuries. It was the official residence of the Habsburgs until 1918.

The oldest buildings, which include the Hofkapelle (the Imperial Chapel), are those round the Schweizerhof (named after Maria Theresia's Swiss guard). They were begun under Ottokar of Bohemia, but the present buildings are from somewhat later. The imperial crown jewels (including the insignia of the Holy Roman Empire and the Order of the Fleece) are still kept in this well-protected part of the castle in the Schatzkammer.

The buildings around the square 'In der Burg' date from different eras. Opposite the Schweizerhof is the Amalienburg, so-called after Joseph

I's widow, who lived here in the 18th century, as did Tsar Alexander during the Viennese Congress, Empress Elisabeth ('Sissy') towards the end of the 19th century and Karl, the last Austro-Hungarian emperor, from 1916 to 1918. This part was built in the 16th and early 17th centuries but was not linked to the rest of the palace until the Leopoldinische Trakt (Leopold Wing) was added more than a century later. It was here that Maria Theresia had her winter residence and the rooms adapted at her command are now occupied by the Austrian president. Construction of the Reichskanzleitrakt according to plans by Johann Lukas von Hildebrandt and Fischer von Erlach began under Karl VI in 1723, joining up the Amalienburg and the Schweizerhof. Emperor Franz Joseph's apartments are in this wing.

The Hofburg continues around the Josefsplatz (see page 31) and includes the Imperial Library and its world famous Prunksaal. This wing was begun in 1723-6 by Johann B. Fischer von Erlach and finished by his son in 1767-73; it includes the large and small Redoute halls and the Spanische Reitschule (Spanish Riding School) (see page 33).

The dome of the Michaelertrakt (St Michael's Wing) dominates the Michaelerplatz and presents one of the most spectacular aspects of the palace. It was built on the site of the old Court Theatre, which had moved to its new building on the Ringstraße. The original plans of Fischer von Erlach were not realized but the architect, Ferdinand Kirschner, based his version in part on the original design and built it in 1889-93 in the romantic historicist style of the Ringstraße era.

The last building phase was in the early 20th century when work was begun on the planned 'Kaiserforum' of which only the Neue Burg (see page 30), the Burgtor (which had been begun in 1821) and the two museums (art gallery and natural history) were ever completed. This wing, with its impressive concave façade, houses the National Library and various museums.

23

PALAIS AUERSPERG 18 L9 U 2 Lerchenfelder Straße
8, Auerspergstraße 1.

Built in the baroque style around 1706, possibly by Johann Lukas von Hildebrandt, the palace was repeatedly altered in the 18th and 19th centuries and some rooms were refurbished in the classical style. There are pretty gardens at the back, with an orangery, near which Beethoven composed his *Missa Solemnis*. Hieronymus Marchese Capece di Rofrano, once the palace's owner, is said to have been the model for Richard Strauss's *Rosenkavalier*.

During the latter part of the Second World War, the palace served as the secret headquarters for the Austrian resistance movement.

PALAIS ESTERHAZY   18/19 M/N9   U 1, U 3 Stephansplatz
1, Wallnerstraße 4.
Built in 1695, this baroque palace was repeatedly altered during the 18th century. Joseph Haydn used to give concerts in its chapel and Mozart often performed here from 1783 to 1789.

PALAIS FERSTEL   18 M10   U 3 Herrengasse
1, Freyung 2/Herrengasse 17.
The Palais Ferstel was designed and built in his usual romantic historicist style by Viennese architect Heinrich Ferstel (who also built the Votivkirche, see page 21) for the Austro-Hungarian Bank between 1856 and 1860. It also housed (and now houses again) the once famous Café Central. It underwent major restoration between 1975 and 1986, and now contains a magnificently decorated arcade of shops. Well worth a visit.

24

PALAIS HARRACH   18 M10   U 3 Herrengasse
1, Freyung.
Built *c.*1690 (probably to a design by Domenico Martinelli), this exemplary baroque palace was repeatedly altered and then badly damaged during the Second World War. Renovation is still not complete. Haydn's mother was family cook here in the 18th century and Mozart performed here with Nannerl in 1762.

PALAIS KINSKY   18 M10   U 3 Herrengasse
1, Freyung 4.
This is one of the main examples of Johann Lukas von Hildebrandt's baroque architecture. It was built between 1713 and 1716 and today houses an arcade of shops and a café.

PALAIS LIECHTENSTEIN   12 M11   Tram D Fürstengasse
9, Fürstengasse 1.
Designed and built between 1698 and 1711 by Domenico Martinello, the palace and the garden are among the most impressive in Vienna, after those owned by the Habsburgs and Prince Eugen. It is still the property of the Liechtenstein family, but now houses parts of the Museum Moderner Kunst (Museum of Modern Art, see page 46).

PALAIS PALFFY   19 N9   U 1, U 3 Stephansplatz
1, Josefsplatz 6.
Built around 1575, the Josefsplatz façade is in the Renaissance style with a classical portico. Mozart frequently performed here, and today the palace is used mainly for concerts, readings, exhibitions and receptions.

It is one of the buildings used in *The Third Man*: the main action of the film begins here. (It is frequently shown at the Burgkino in summer – try to see it and then go 'sight-hunting' afterwards!)

PALAIS SCHWARZENBERG   19 N/O8   Tram D Gußhausstraße 3, Rennweg 2.

When it was built, between 1697 and 1704, this baroque palace was well outside the city walls; but it was next to Prince Eugen's Belvedere Palace, which tempted other aristocrats to follow suit. The Schwarzenberg Palace was executed by the top names of the time: originally designed by Johann Lukas von Hildebrandt, with alterations and additions by Fischer von Erlach and frescos by Daniel Gran. Today, one wing, still Schwarzenberg property, has been converted into a luxury hotel.

SCHLOß SCHÖNBRUNN   22 H7   U 4 Schönbrunn

13, Schönbrunner Schloßstraße 13; tel. 81 11 13. Open April to October daily 8.30 a.m.–5.30 p.m.; November to March daily 9 a.m.–4 p.m. Only the Gala rooms can be seen, on guided tours. These are held daily in German and English. Other languages (French, Italian and Spanish) depending on the season and availability of guides.

25

Schönbrunn, Austria's answer to Versailles, is one of the most magnificent secular baroque buildings in Vienna and should not be missed. The palace is surrounded by exquisitely laid out gardens and a park that contains one of the few remaining baroque zoos in the world, a magnificent palm house and the Gloriette, a triumphal arch on top of a hill overlooking the city.

Of the 1441 rooms in the palace, only 45 are open to the public but many of these have seen momentous history: in the Blue Chinese Salon Emperor Karl was forced to relinquish any participation in the affairs of the state (although contrary to popular belief he never abdicated), thus bringing 640 years of Habsburg rule to a close in 1918; the six-year-old child prodigy Mozart performed in the Hall of Mirrors and proposed to the Empress's ill-fated daughter, Marie Antoinette, to her great amusement; Napoleon discussed his campaign with his generals in the Vieux Laque Room in 1809; the Grand Gallery is where the Congress of Austria danced its way to diplomacy in 1814-15 and where state receptions are still held today for visiting heads of state. Most of the rooms are decorated in the rococo style, the most spectacular example being the Room of Millions, which is panelled with rosewood and decorated with 60 Indo-Persian miniatures dating from the 16th and 17th centuries. However, the rooms used by Franz Joseph, who was born and spent the last years of his life here, are unpretentiously furnished.

There is enough to see in Schönbrunn palace and park to warrant an entire day's visit, but take some refreshment with you as cafés are few and prices are high.

STADTPALAIS LIECHTENSTEIN 18 M9   U 3 Herrengasse
1, Bankgasse 2.
Still owned by the princes of Liechtenstein, like the Palais Liechtenstein, the town palace was also built to a design by Domenico Martinello but was substantially altered whilst under construction in 1694-1706. The ostentatious baroque building has a remarkable portico.

THE RINGSTRAßE

If you only have one day to spend in Vienna, an ideal way of seeing many of the main sights of the city is to walk, cycle or take a tram ride round the Ringstraße, the boulevard that encircles the inner city – the First District. Trams 1 and 2 both do this circuit.

26

BÖRSE 18/19 M/N10   Tram 1, 2 Börse
1, Schottenring 16.
Built 1874-7 by Theophil Hansen, the building is still in use as the Vienna stock exchange, but the once richly adorned main hall burnt out in 1956 and was converted into a courtyard.

BURGTHEATER 18 M9   Tram 1, 2 Burgtheater/Rathaus
1, Dr-Karl-Lueger-Ring 2.
The Burgtheater is the second oldest stage in the world, having been founded by Maria Theresia in 1741. The present building dates from 1874–88 and its style is reminiscent of the Italian Renaissance. Together with the opera house, the Burgtheater was the model for dozens of theatre buildings, albeit on a smaller scale, all over the Austro-Hungarian Empire. Partly destroyed in Allied air raids in 1945, it was beautifully restored soon afterwards and is again one of the most important stages in the German-speaking world.

HELDENPLATZ, NEUE BURG, BURGTOR (See page 30.)

KRIEGSMINISTERIUM 19 O9   U 3 Stubentor
1, Stubenring 1.
The former War Ministry was built in 1909-13 in a neo-baroque style, typical of the romantic historicism of other buildings on the Ring. Its main

claim is its stark contrast to the 'modern' Postsparkassenamt (Post Office Savings Bank) built by Otto Wagner across the boulevard (see page 36).

KUNSTHISTORISCHES MUSEUM (See page 42.)

NATURHISTORISCHES MUSEUM (See page 44.)

ÖSTERREICHISCHES MUSEUM FÜR ANGEWANDTE KUNST (See page 45.)

PARLAMENT **18** M9   Tram 1, 2 Parlament
1, Dr-Karl-Renner-Ring.
Built between 1874 and 1884 by Theophil Hansen, in a style reminiscent of a Greek temple, the parliament building was used by the Reichsrat (Council of the Empire) for the Austrian half of the Austro-Hungarian Empire until 1918. Nowadays it is the seat of both the National Council, whose representatives are directly elected by the people, and also the Federal Council, whose members are delegated by the individual counties.

27

POSTSPARKASSENAMT (See page 37.)

RATHAUS **18** M9/10   Tram 1, 2 Burgtheater/Rathaus
1, Rathausplatz 1.
The town hall was built 1872–83 in neo-Gothic style by Friedrich Schmidt, the master-builder of Cologne Cathedral. It is distinguished by the 321ft (98m) central tower, adorned by an 11ft (3.4m) flag-bearing metal knight: the 'Rathausmann', symbol of the traditionally Socialist city council.

    The Rathaus is the seat of the mayor (and governor) of Vienna and houses many council offices as well as the city and county archive and library. The ample building has a beautiful large arcaded courtyard, which in summer is a delightful setting for concerts and other functions. The Schmidthalle, the spacious entrance hall at the back of the building (Rathausstraße), contains the City Information Office, which is not primarily tourist orientated, despite being the meeting point for many guided tours run by the City Council.

ROßAUERKASERNE **12/13** M/N10/11   U 2, U 4 Schottenring
9, Schlickplatz 6/Maria-Theresienstraße 21–23/Roßauerlände 1/-Türkenstraße 22.
This building is just off the Ringstraße but is well worth a short detour. These red-brick army barracks (now part of police headquarters) were built in 1865-9 in the style of a medieval castle.

STAATSOPER **19** N8 Tram D, 1, 2 Oper
1, Opernring 2. Staatsoper; tel. 514 44-2959. Guided tours available.
The State Opera is one of the three leading opera houses in the world
and plays to full houses almost every night of its season (1 September
to 30 June). It is also one of the largest opera houses in Europe, with a
capacity of 2,209. The list of directors includes many of the great musicians of this century: Gustav Mahler, Richard Strauss, Karl Böhm and
Herbert von Karajan.

Built in a 'free' Renaissance style, the opera house was one of the first
major buildings on the Ringstraße to be completed. It opened in 1869
with Mozart's *Don Giovanni* and continued to play with few interruptions
until it was all but destroyed by Allied bombs on 12 March 1945. It was
rebuilt from 1945-55. (See page 107.)

UNIVERSITÄT **18** M10 U 2 Schottentor
1, Dr-Karl-Lueger-Ring 1; tel. 40103-0.

28 Vienna University was founded in 1365 and is the oldest in any German-
speaking country. It was originally housed in the eastern corner of the
inner city. This is another splendid building by Heinrich Ferstel, again
influenced by the Italian Renaissance. Despite substantial war damage
it was rebuilt and is still in use as the main building of Vienna University,
housing the University library as well as parts of the arts faculty. The fes-
tive hall of the University is richly decorated with frescoes by G. Klimt
and the arcaded courtyard contains monuments to many outstanding
scientists and scholars.

VOTIVKIRCHE (See page 21.)

TOWN HOUSES

One of the best pieces of advice for a visitor to Vienna is to keep your
eyes well above street level. There are so many beautiful houses, and
so many delightful features on otherwise uninspiring buildings, that you
will find out far more by keeping your eyes peeled than by reading any
guide book. However, so that you do not miss the most famous places,
here are a few suggestions. (Also, some of the most magnificent town
houses are to be found in the charming Old University Quarter.)

ANKERHAUS **19** N9 U 1, U 3 Stephansplatz
1, Graben 10 (= Spiegelgasse 2).
This carefully constructed building with the glassed-over ground floors

and its roof atelier (at present lived in by Friedensreich Hundertwasser) was designed by Otto Wagner for the Anker insurance company in 1894.

DREIMÄDERLHAUS **18** M10   U 2 Schottentor
1, Schreyvogelgasse 10.
Built in 1803, this is a fine example of an upper-middle-class private house from the beginning of the 19th century, its unostentatious beauty being a typical feature of the Biedermeier period. Its name (Three Maidens' House), which suggests a link to the composer Franz Schubert, is the result of pure legend.

FIGAROHAUS **19** N9   U 1, U 3 Stefansplatz
1, Domgasse 5 (= Schulerstraße 8). Museum opening times: Tuesday to Friday 10 a.m.–4 p.m., Saturday 2–6 p.m., Sunday 9 a.m.–1 p.m.
This five-storeyed house was built in 1716. Its claim to fame is that Mozart lived in a flat here from 1784 to 1787 and composed the *Marriage of Figaro*, seven piano concertos and the Haydn quartets. Several composers visited him at this flat, notably Haydn and Beethoven. The house is now a museum owned by the city.

29

PASQUALATIHAUS **18** M10   U 2 Schottentor
1, Mölker Bastei 8.
The house itself is a fairly inconspicuous building from 1797, but the owner, Pasqualati, was a great admirer of Beethoven, so the composer spent a lot of time here, writing, among other works, *Fidelio*, symphonies 4, 5 and 7, his violin concerto and several quartets. The building now houses a Beethoven museum (see also page 50). Another famous name connected with the house is that of novelist Adalbert Stifter.

SQUARES

Possibly more so than in any other city, Vienna's history and everyday life seems to exist around its squares.

AM HOF **19** N10   U 3 Herrengasse
1, Am Hof.
This splendid square, opening out suddenly from the narrow streets surrounding it, has been significant throughout history. The buildings that line it today are for the most part from the 17th and 18th century. The balcony of the impressive Church Am Hof was the platform for one of Hitler's first speeches to jubilant Nazi crowds beneath him. In 1983 Pope

John Paul II used the same balcony to greet thousands of Croatians and other foreign visitors on his visit to the capital.

FREYUNG **18** M10   U 2 Schottentor
1, Freyung.
Entering the city from the Schottentor and going down the Schottengasse and part of the Herrengasse, that narrow road dissecting the inner city, the Freyung opens up in front of you. The buildings all around are spectacular: on one side are ornate palaces such as Palais Kinsky (see page 24), Palais Harrach (see page 24) and Palais Ferstel (see page 24), and on the other the towering Benedictine Schottenkirche (see page 19).

GRABEN **19** N9   U1 Stephansplatz
1, Graben.
This wide pedestrian precinct occupies the site of the ditch that fortified the Roman camp. It was later a meat and then a vegetable market. The Graben has seen many court and church festivals – the annual Corpus Christi procession still moves down here *en route* to the cathedral.

There are several interesting sights here, notably the Pestsäule (Plague Column), an impressively decorated baroque column that was erected in the late 17th century at the instigation of Leopold I, in gratitude for the city's deliverance from the Black Death.

At the corner of the Graben and the Kärtnerstraße is the Stock im Eisen (stick set in iron). This was first mentioned in 1533, and legend has it that locksmith apprentices would hammer a nail into the stump before leaving the city. The supposedly unopenable lock around it was discovered on closer examination to be a pure fake.

HELDENPLATZ,   Tram 1, 2 Babenbergerstraße
NEUE BURG AND BURGTOR **18** M9
1, Heldenplatz.
Nowhere in Vienna is more beautiful than the wide expanse of the Heldenplatz (the Square of the Heroes). The concave wing of the Hofburg, known as the Neue Burg (New Palace), forms one side of the Heldenplatz. It was built at the turn of the century as part of Gottfried Semper's Kaiserforum (Imperial Forum), which was to include a mirror-image counterpart to the Neue Burg and triumphal arches linking it to the museums over the Ring. Only the two facing equestrian statues suggest that a wing of the palace is missing.

The Burgtor (Castle Gate), which was built from 1821 to 1824, marked the limits of the city towards the glacis, the area in front of the city walls that prior to the construction of the Ringstraße had been left open for military purposes. The gate was rebuilt into Austria's Monument to the Unknown Soldier in 1933-4.

On 15 March 1938 the Heldenplatz was the site of a rally held by Hitler to mark the annexation of Austria by Nazi Germany. A metal cross next to the gate commemorates the visit to Vienna of Pope John Paul II in 1983.

HOHER MARKT   19 N9/10   U 1, U 3 Stephansplatz
1, Hoher Markt.

Because of bomb damage in the Second World War, this square appears to be quite modern. However, it is the site of part of the Roman camp and the ruins of the praetorium are among the finds open to visitors. As its name suggests, the square was at one time the centre of the medieval town with its market, court and pillory. It was even the site of executions, the last public execution here occurring in 1703.

The fountain in the centre of the square is known as the Vermählungs-brunnen (Marriage Fountain) as the pillar portrays the marriage of St Joseph to Our Lady. The highly decorated clock spanning the space between two buildings over the Judengasse is the Ankeruhr.

31

JOSEFSPLATZ   19 N9   U 1, U 3 Stephansplatz
1, Josefsplatz.

This square is created by wings of the Hofburg, housing the Prunksaal of the National Library (said to be the most beautiful library room in the world), the Spanische Reitschule (Spanish Riding School) (see page 33) and the Augustinerkirche (see page 16). The central statue of Joseph II imitates the statue of the Roman Emperor Marcus Aurelius on the Capitol in Rome. Facing the statue is Palais Palffy (see page 24).

Joseph II

Joseph II did much to improve the lives of his subjects. The emperor who wished to have the words: 'Here lies Joseph II who failed in everything he undertook' inscribed on his coffin also declared : 'In any empire over which I rule, government must be according to my principles – prejudice, fanaticism, partiality and slavery must disappear so that everyone of my subjects can enjoy the freedom which he was born to.' Joseph II did indeed abolish slavery within his Empire, as well as granting increased religious freedom to both Protestants and Jews and introducing other social benefits, such as the opening of public parks like the Prater.

NEUER MARKT **19** N9   U 1, U 3 Stephansplatz
1, Neuer Markt.
This square was the centre of the 'new town' development of around 1200. Over the centuries it became a popular place of entertainment, until the Capuchins put an end to that by building their monastery and imperial crypt there at the beginning of the 17th century. The houses and shops lining the square are elegant and pleasing to the eye, but the square's dominating feature is the Donnerbrunnen (Donner Fountain), named after its designer, Georg Raphael Donner. It was created between 1737 and 1739 and depicts Providence at the centre, with allegorical figures of the rivers Traun, Enns, Ybbs and March (all tributaries of the Danube) around it.

RUPRECHTSPLATZ **19** N10   U 2, U 4 Schwedenplatz
1, Ruprechtsplatz.
This was originally the marketplace and centre of the tiny village that was Vienna after the Romans had left. It contains Ruprechtskirche, the oldest and one of the smallest churches in the city.

32

SCHWARZENBERGPLATZ **19** N/O8   Tram 1, 2,
1, Schwarzenbergplatz.   D Schwarzenbergplatz
This square, which is close to the Palais Schwarzenberg (see page 25) and the Belvedere (see page 21), was in the Russian zone after the war. At that time it was called Stalin Square and a memorial to Russian soldiers of the Second World War was erected there.

SIGMUND FREUD PARK **12** M10   U 2 Schottentor
1, Sigmund Freud Park.
The park in front of the Votivkirche now honours the famous Viennese father of psychoanalysis. The history of the names given to this square over the years shows something of the chameleon character of the Austrians. It was first called Maximilianplatz after the instigator of the Votivkirche, then after 1919 it was Freedom Square, in 1934 it became Dollfuß Square (after the right-wing premier), in 1938 Göring Square, in 1945 Freedom Square, in 1946 Roosevelt Square and, finally, in 1985 it was given its present name. Who's next?

STEPHANSPLATZ **19** N9   U 1, U 3 Stephansplatz
1, Stephansplatz.
Until 1732, the area around the cathedral was taken up by the graveyard and various houses. Now there is a mixture of magnificent older buildings and more modern ones. The Haas-Haus (see page 35), the

shopping centre mirroring the cathedral in its glass front, is one of the more highly disputed modern additions.

OTHER SIGHTS

MUSIKVEREIN   **19** N8   U 1, U 2, U 4 Karlsplatz
1, Bösendorferstraße.
This home of the Vienna Philharmonic Orchestra was designed by Theophil von Hansen in the Greek Renaissance style, and audiences have packed in to hear the world-famous orchestra play in the Golden Concert Hall since 1870. The hall is familiar to many from the annual live coverage of the New Year's Day concert. Each year in late January the seating is removed and the parquet floor becomes, for one evening, one of Vienna's best ballrooms for dancing to the world-famous Strauss waltzes.

33

    Philharmonic concerts are traditionally held on Saturday afternoons and Sunday mornings.

RIESENRAD   **14** P10   U 1 Praterstern
2, Praterstern.
The Riesenrad (Giant Ferris Wheel) is not only a landmark for the Prater (see page 143) but also for the whole of Vienna, especially since it featured in *The Third Man*. It was built in 1896-7 by an English engineer, Walter B. Basset, for the World Exhibition held in Vienna, and we are extremely lucky that it is still here, as similar constructions in London, Blackpool and Paris were sold for scrap.

    The wheel is 209ft (64.75m) high and has a diameter of 197ft (61m). It travels round at the very relaxed speed of 2ft 6in (0.75m) per second, with repeated stops to allow people to enter the cabins, so you have plenty of time to enjoy the view of Vienna and the Prater from the top. A ride on it is certainly among the main attractions of the city.

SPANISCHE REITSCHULE   U 1, U 3 Stephansplatz
(WINTERREITSCHULE)   **19** N9
1, Josefsplatz. The Lippizaner horses can be watched in training (after a period of queuing!) from February to June and from September to mid-December (Tuesday to Saturday 10 a.m.–12 noon) but for performances tickets must be ordered well in advance.
This building dates from the beginning of the 18th century (1729-35) and was commissioned by Karl VI for great galas and fêtes. During the

Congress of Vienna it was the scene of magnificent festivals. However, the main purpose of the elegant large hall was to exercise horses and maintain riding skills during winter. It has served the art of Spanish riding since it was built and is still the place where the celebrated Spanish Riding School performs.

ZENTRALFRIEDHOF
Tram 71, 72 Zentralfriedhof 3. Tor
11, Simmeringer Hauptstraße 232–244.
When Vienna rapidly expanded during the second half of the 19th century and the district graveyards became too small, it was decided to lay out a huge central cemetery, which opened in 1874. It includes a Jewish section (Gate 1), a major church, a section for official burials, a tomb for the presidents of the republic, a grove of honour and a crematorium, erected in 1922 by Clemens Holzmeister. This crematorium, built in an oriental, fort-like style in the grounds of the Schloß Neugebäude is not the only architecturally interesting feature of the graveyard: the main entrance (Gate 2) is executed in the *Jugendstil*, and so is the Kirche am Zentralfriedhof (also called Dr Karl Lueger Memorial Church in honour of a former mayor of Vienna interred there). The most interesting feature to the visitor will be the Grove of Honour, which contains either the actual graves of, or – as in the case of Mozart – memorials to many famous artists, e.g. the composers Beethoven, Gluck, Schubert, Brahms, Strauss and Schönberg, to name but a few.

34

ARCHITECTURE

ALTES RATHAUS   **19** N10
Tram 1, 2 Börse
1, Wipplingerstraße 8.
This early-14th-century building was originally a private house. It was confiscated by the Habsburgs after a plot against them (in 1309) and given to the city. It was used as a town hall right to the end of the 19th century, when the new town hall on the Ring was built. The façade is an 18th-century addition, and the fountain in the courtyard (*Andromeda-brunnen*) is the work of G.R. Donner and dates from 1741. The building now houses various museums (see MUSEUMS) and rooms for exhibitions and functions.

CENTRAL REFUSE INCINERATOR   **12** M12   U 6 Nußdorfer Straße
19, Spittelauer Lände.
Are you surprised that we should suggest you look at this? Friedensreich

Hundertwasser was the architect and, as with his Hundertwasserhaus (see below), greenery and decoration are much in evidence. It is colourful, amusing and it is a functioning refuse incinerator, though you might not guess it. His critics, the supporters of modern architecture, feel it is not true to its function. See what you think.

GROẞES MICHAELERHAUS   19 N9   U 3 Herrengasse
1, Kohlmarkt 11.
This 18th-century house's most famous occupant was Joseph Haydn, who lived here for several years from 1750, together with his teacher Porpora. Legend has it that Haydn moved here after he had been dismissed from the Boys' Choir when his father had thwarted his plans to allow himself to be castrated to preserve his beautiful treble voice.

HAAS-HAUS   19 N9   U 1, U 3 Stephansplatz
1, Stephansplatz 12.
Built in 1985-9 by Hans Hollein, his first prominent building in the city. Major and extended discussions took place before Hollein's much modified plans were finally approved. The building has an undeniable presence and extraordinary quality of workmanship and materials. It still provokes discussion today.

HUNDERTWASSERHAUS   20 P9   Tram N Hetzgasse
3, Löwengasse 41–3.
The foundation stone for this truly spectacular and very colourful house was laid in 1983. Hundertwasser's plans were to make the structure of the building as open as possible and to use as many plants as possible. Hundertwasser is an artist who has involved himself heavily in Vienna's architecture. and provokes much discussion.

JURIDICUM   18 M10   U 2 Schottentor
1, Schottenbastei 10–16.
It took E. Hiesmayr from 1969 to 1983 to build this University Faculty of Law. The method – a hanging construction of steel columns filled with liquid – was innovative and interesting. The fact that it would no longer be allowed in this location because of Vienna's conservationist lobby also adds interest, as does the lack of attention paid by the architects to the actual needs of the users.

LOOS-HAUS   18/19 M/N9   U 3 Herrengasse
1, Michaelerplatz 3.
Built in 1910-11, this house is on a very prominent corner of the city and

provoked great controversy. Its clean façade broke drastically with the historicist and baroque-type building in Vienna at the turn of the century and paved the way for boring 20th-century façades.

RETTI CANDLE SHOP   19 N9   U 3 Herrengasse
1, Kohlmarkt 10.
Shop fronts seem to be the means of expression for Vienna's small group of modern architects. Take care to look at the designs – this one was Hans Hollein's first building project in 1964-5.

UNO-CITY   U 1 Kaisermühlen
(VIENNA INTERNATIONAL CENTRE)   14 R2
22, Wagramer Straße/Donaupark.
This landmark of modern Vienna was built in 1973-9 in the hope of attracting various UN offices to Vienna. Today the IAEA and UNIDO have their main seats in the city. The somewhat controversial building conglomerate consists of four towers up to 394ft (120m) high with concave fronts and a total of 24,000 windows. Next door to it is the lower-lying, but still huge, complex of the Vienna Austrian Centre, also called the Conference Centre. UNO-City is rented from the Republic of Austria for a fee of one schilling per annum!

36

VOLKSSCHULE   Tram 40, 41 Weinhausergasse
IN DER KÖHLERGASSE   11 J12
18, Köhlergasse.
Completed in 1991, this Hans Hollein project is immediately pleasing to the eye. His use of colour and simplicity of forms make distinct reference to earlier buildings on the site and are at once modern and retro.

ENGEL APOTHEKE   19 N9   U 1, U 3 Stephansplatz
1, Bognergasse 9.
This narrow town house was built in 1901 by O. Laske, a pupil of Otto Wagner. It contains a chemist's on the ground floor and has an excellent art nouveau façade, with a mosaic of two angels – hence the name.

OTTO WAGNER-VILLA I   Tram 49 Bujattigasse
(ERNST FUCHS PRIVATMUSEUM)
14, Hüttelbergstraße 28; tel. 94 75 86. Daily 9.30 a.m.–3.30 p.m.

OTTO WAGNER-VILLA II   Tram 49 Bujattigasse
14, Hüttelbergstraße 26; tel. 94 75 86.
As improbable a pair of suburban villas as you are likely to see. Designed

by Otto Wagner, they stand side by side on the edge of the Höhenstraße at Hütteldorf. They are so unexpected in that setting that you can't miss them, despite the tall trees lining the road.

The Villa Wagner I was built in 1886-8 as Wagner's summer house, and occupied by him between 1895 and 1912. It is essentially Palladian and is immediately striking because of the grandeur of its scale, emphasized by its position on a slight slope above the road. It is from Wagner's earlier historicist period and shows the powerful influence of the Renaissance. The house is now a private museum, exhibiting works by Ernst Fuchs, the present owner, himself a leading figure of Vienna's artistic establishment.

Wagner built Villa Wagner II in 1912-13, after he sold the Villa I. It is not in such good condition as the other, but is the least altered of the pair of villas and more representative of the work for which Wagner is famous. It is not open to the public, but from the outside it is clear that it reflects Wagner's later functionalist approach as well as developments in society's attitudes to housing.

37

POSTSPARKASSENAMT   **19** O9   U 1, 4 Schwedenplatz
1, Georg Coch-Platz 2.
The Post Office Savings Bank was designed by Otto Wagner and built from 1904 to 1906 using the most modern materials and constructional methods available. The clear-cut, functional exterior and representative hall inside were in sharp contrast to the historicism dominant in the architecture of the time and, indeed, in Wagner's earlier period.

U-BAHN-STATION   U 4 Kettenbrückengasse
KETTENBRÜCKENGASSE   **18** M8
5/6, Linke Wienzeile.
In 1892-1903, when the Stadtbahn was built, it was a very advanced transport system. Both planning and design were executed by Otto Wagner, so it was not only functional, but also very pretty and heavily influenced by art nouveau.

OTHER *JUGENDSTIL* BUILDINGS
3, Dannebergplatz 11.   **19** P8   Tram O Neulinggasse
This block of flats was built in 1906 and shows a strong Secessionist influence. The doorway is a *Jugendstil* masterpiece.
3, Ungargasse 59–61.   **19** P8   Tram O Neulinggasse
This office building belonging to a furniture firm was one of the first utilitarian buildings in Vienna to be built with art nouveau features, in this case an exquisite tiled façade.

6, Köstlergasse 3.   **18** M8   U 4 Kettenbrückengasse
An art nouveau patrician house designed by Otto Wagner, simple and
economic in form, yet beautiful in its design.

6, Linke Wienzeile 38.   **18** M8   U 4 Kettenbrückengasse
A magnificent art nouveau patrician house, executed by leading
Viennese *Jugendstil* artists (gold medallions on the façade by Kolo
Moser, sculptures by O. Schimkowitz), with superb wrought-ironwork in
the stairwell. It is one of the finest examples of art nouveau architecture.

6, Linke Wienzeile 40.   **18** M8   U 4 Kettenbrückengasse
The Majolikahaus was built in 1888-9 according to plans by Otto Wagner
and takes its name from the floral tile design that is used on the façade.
The only relief elements are the lionheads.

6, Linke Wienzeile 48-52.   **18** M8   U 4 Kettenbrückengasse
Built in 1913, this office block introduced a new element into Viennese
architecture, namely the bay windows flanked by columns in the upper
floors. The house also has a remarkable stairwell.

38

Jugendstil

There are two principal styles of art that are hard to avoid in Vienna,
one is the baroque and the other is *Jugendstil*, or art nouveau.
Jugendstil appeared more or less simultaneously in French painting and English applied art in the 1880s and the trend continued until the outbreak of the First World War. In Austria it really caught the
imagination of the art world and the result was the foundation of the
Secession by a group of renegade artists from the Academy in 1897.
The central figure of the Secession was Gustav Klimt, whose erotic,
fairy-tale-like painting and themes came to embody *Jugendstil* for
many. Other important names are the artist and designer Koloman
Moser, and architects Otto Wagner and Josef Hoffmann.

The style, which uses linear, often asymmetric, decoration of floral or geometric origin, still has a great influence in Austria today. The
number of antique shops specializing in *Jugendstil* indicates this.

In many ways *Jugendstil* was less of an art style and more of a
way of life, as it tried not only to create a unity of the arts (the artists
were architects, graphic artists, painters, designers, illustrators, etc.)
but also a unity between art and life. This can be seen most clearly
in the work of Otto Wagner, who believed in the linking of function
and aesthetic. His architectural designs for buildings and bridges
(for example, the Stadtbahn, now U-bahn) were detailed even down
to the appearance and positioning of nuts and bolts, each with significant functional and aesthetic roles.

Red Vienna

The five-fold growth of Vienna in the 19th century was due to belated industrialization and the subsequent immigration of thousands of people from different parts of the Empire to find work in the new factories. There was suddenly a terrible housing shortage, and by 1900 half of the population had to live in tiny flats – in the workers' districts a kitchen and one room had to suffice for a whole family and often the kitchen would be rented out by the night to a worker.

The end of the Austro-Hungarian Empire in 1918 brought with it changes in the social structure of the now tiny country, with its population drastically reduced from 50 million to 6½ million, 2 million of whom lived in the capital. The workers had already been organizing themselves into political bodies during the final decades of the previous century, now the process accelerated.

One of the main founders of the First Republic (1918–38) was the Viennese Social Democrat Karl Renner. He and his council established a building programme aimed at creating 60,000 new flats in 10 years. This, together with other council projects, such as a new school system and various other adult educational programmes, nurseries and a better health and hygiene system, revolutionized the lives of the workers. Vienna became the paradigm of socialism, earning itself the name 'Red Vienna'.

The council employed leading architects such as Adolf Loos and Josef Hoffmann to design their housing schemes. *Mietkasernen* (rent-barracks) were created – huge, fortress-like buildings consisting of small flats, all with outside windows and running water, built around large, airy, green courtyards. In addition, each complex had nurseries and clubs for the Socialist party.

During the civil war of 1934, several of the building complexes were the sites of pitched battles against the police. The crushing of civil unrest and the subsequent prohibition of the Socialist party smoothed the path of the Nazi takeover. The main housing complexes are:

Karl-Marx-Hof U 4, U 6 Heiligenstadt
19, Heiligenstädter Straße 82-92.

Matzleinsthaler Hof S 1, S 2 Matzleinsdorfer Platz
5, Margaretengürtel 90–98..

Rabenhof 🚌 77A Kardinal Nagl-Platz
3, Rabengasse 1–9 and 2–12/Baumgasse 29–41.

Seitz-Hof 🚌 36A Bellgasse
21, Jedleseer Straße 66–94.

Whatever the topic, Vienna has a museum or exhibition for it: either in the impressively large collections of the national museums or in the smaller and lesser-known museums in the suburbs. Many of the larger museums are based on imperial collections once belonging to the Habsburgs, and have changed little in their style of presentation. Opening hours can be somewhat idiosyncratic, so always check in advance.

HISTORICAL AND ART MUSEUMS

AKADEMIE DER BILDENDEN KÜNSTE: GEMÄLDEGALERIE 18 M8 U 1, U 2, U 4 Karlsplatz, Tram 1, 2 Oper

1, Schillerplatz 3; tel. 588 16-0. Tuesday, Thursday, Friday 10 a.m.–2 p.m., Wednesday 10 a.m.–1 p.m., 4–6 p.m., Saturday, Sunday 9 a.m.–1 p.m.
Partly based on paintings submitted by members of the academy, the collection was substantially enlarged by other donations and now has a larger proportion of 16th- and 17th-century Dutch, German and Italian works, including paintings by Bosch, Grien, Cranach, Rubens, van Dyck, Rembrandt and Titian.

41

ERZBISCHÖFLICHES DOM- UND DIÖZESANMUSEUM 19 N9 U 1, U 3 Stephansplatz

1, Stephansplatz 6; tel. 513 25 61. Wednesday to Saturday 10 a.m.– 4 p.m., Sunday and Holidays 10 a.m.–1 p.m.
This is basically the cathedral treasury with a fine collection of 13th–19th-century religious art, but it also contains unexpected items, such as a good selection of 20th-century graphic art.

GRAPHISCHE SAMMLUNG ALBERTINA 19 N9 Tram 1, 2 Oper

1, Augustinerstraße 1; tel. 534 83-0. Exhibition: Monday, Tuesday, Thursday 10 a.m.–4 p.m., Wednesday 10 a.m.–6 p.m., Friday 10 a.m.–2 p.m., Saturday, Sunday 10 a.m.–1 p.m. Closed Sunday in July and August. Reading Room: Monday to Thursday 1–4 p.m., Closed July and August.
The collections of the copper-plate engravings of the *Kupferstichkabinett der Kaiserlichen Hofbibliothek* (Imperial Court Library) and Duke Albert

The Austrian Gallery of 19ᵗʰ and 20ᵗʰ Century Art is housed in the upper palace of the Belvedere.

of Saxe-Teschen (1738–1822) were combined on the latter's initiative to form one of the largest collections of graphic art, commonly called 'The Albertina', containing 1.5 million graphic prints and 44,000 paintings as well as a library of 50,000 volumes. The prints include works by Dürer, Leonardo da Vinci, Michelangelo, Rafael, Rubens and Rembrandt as well as many modern artists. Only a relatively small number are exhibited in the reading room, and the exhibitions vary. Unfortunately, most items permanently on display are reproductions, in order to preserve the originals.

HISTORISCHES MUSEUM DER STADT WIEN

1 HISTORISCHES MUSEUM DER STADT WIEN (MAIN BUILDING) **18** N8
U 1, U 2, U 4 Karlsplatz

4, Karlsplatz/Maderstraße; tel. 505 87 47-0. Daily except Monday 9 a.m–4.30 p.m. Closed 1 January, 1 May, 25 December.
This main building of the Historical Museum of the City of Vienna houses, as you might expect, relics and documents of the history of Vienna from prehistoric times to the present. More importantly, though, the museum is also responsible for the upkeep of many of the remains and monuments you come across in Vienna, such as the Roman excavations in the city and a number of artists' memorial rooms. The museum also stages widely publicized major exhibitions.

2 HERMESVILLA
Tram 60 and 🚌 60B Lainzer Tor

13, Lainzer Tiergarten (Lainzer Tor); tel. 804 13 24. Wednesday to Sunday and Holidays 9 a.m.–4.30 p.m. Closed 1 January, 1 May, 25 December.
Now part of the Historical Museum of the City of Vienna, the Hermesvilla was once the private mansion belonging to Empress Elisabeth (see Lainzer Tiergarten, page 142). Apart from small exhibitions held annually, the building is interesting for its original furnishings, including a richly decorated imperial gymnastics room, documenting the Empress's love of sports.

KUNSTHISTORISCHES MUSEUM

1 KUNSTHISTORISCHES MUSEUM, HAUPTGEBÄUDE (MAIN BUILDING) **18** M9
U 2 Babenbergerstraße.

1, Burgring 5; tel. 93 45 41-0, 93 44 48-0. Tuesday to Friday 10 a.m.–6 p.m., Saturday and Sunday 9 a.m.–6 p.m. Closed Monday.
Vienna's main art museum is to your left as you stand facing the statue of Maria Theresia with your back to the Hofburg. It was built by Gottfried Semper and Karl von Hasenauerin in 1872–81, in the style of the Italian

42

Renaissance, like all the other majestic buildings along the Ringstraße. The main building now houses Austria's foremost picture gallery (Gemäldegalerie), a classical art collection (Antike Sammlung), an Egyptian–Oriental collection (Ägyptische Sammlung), and a collection of sculptures and decorative art (Sammlung für Plastik und Kunstgewerbe), but the museum also has collections at other sites all over Vienna (listed below).

The Gemäldegalerie exhibits many of the most famous artists with some wonderful works by Titian, Dürer, Rubens and a spectacular collection of Brueghels. Sadly, lack of space prevents all the pictures owned by the museum from being on view at all times, but whenever you go, you will be delighted by the representative cross-section of European art.

2 EPHESOS MUSEUM   **18** M9   Tram 1, 2 Babenbergerstraße

1, Neue Burg, Heldenplatz; tel. 93 45 41-0. Monday, Wednesday, Friday 10 a.m.–4 p.m. Saturday and Sunday 9 a.m.–4 p.m. Closed Tuesday.
A rich collection of classical treasures and architectural finds from the Austrian excavations in Ephesos in Asia minor (Turkey), begun in 1873 and still continuing. The emphasis today is on reconstruction and research rather than on removing objects from the site.

43

3 HOFJAGD-
UND RÜSTKAMMER   **18** M9   Tram 1, 2 Babenbergerstraße

1, Neue Burg, Heldenplatz; tel. 93 45 41-0. Monday, Wednesday, Friday 10 a.m.–4 p.m. Saturday and Sunday 9 a.m.–4 p.m. Closed Tuesday.
The Neue Burg not only houses the Ephesos Museum and the more modern sections of the National Library, but also the biggest and most varied western European collection of late medieval and early modern arms and armour. Founded in 1540 by Frederick III, it contains a lot of ceremonial armour, as well as booty taken from the Turkish armies during the sieges of Vienna in the 16th and 17th centuries.

4 MUSIKINSTRUMENTENSAMMLUNG   **18** M9
Tram 1, 2 Babenbergerstraße

1, Neue Burg, Heldenplatz; tel. 93 45 41-0. Monday, Wednesday, Friday 10 a.m.–4 p.m. Saturday and Sunday 9 a.m.–4 p.m. Closed Tuesday.
This collection not only includes many examples of Renaissance and baroque instruments but also documents the development of musical instruments. Music lovers will be delighted to see the pianos that once belonged to Beethoven, Schumann, Brahms and Mahler, and other instruments once played by Haydn and Schubert.

5 SCHATZKAMMER, WELTLICHE UND GEISTLICHE **18** M9

U 3 Herrengasse

1, Hofburg, Schweizerhof; tel. 521 77-0. Daily except Tuesday 10 a.m.–6 p.m.

The Imperial Treasury has recently found new quarters in the Schweizerhof, the innermost court of the Burg near the Hofburgkapelle. The rooms, still not very spacious, offer a more adequate setting for one of the most interesting collections of treasures in the world. Historically it is unrivalled, holding the crown insignia of the Holy Roman Empire from its earliest Carolingian days to this century, the Austrian imperial crown, a host of treasures from the Burgundian dukedom and the insignia of the Order of the Holy Fleece (including the Golden Fleece itself), to name just a few of the secular treasures.

6 WAGENBURG **22** G/H7

U 4 Schönbrunn.

13, Schloß Schönbrunn; tel. 877 32 44, 87 71 033. Daily except Monday 10 a.m.–5 p.m. (4 p.m. in winter).

The Imperial Coach Collection includes more than 100 coaches, carriages, sleighs and litters from the 17th century to 1916. The most famous is the Habsburg funereal coach, used in 1916 for the funeral of Emperor Franz Joseph and then again, probably for the last time ever, for the funeral of Empress Zita, which took place in 1989.

44

NATURHISTORISCHES MUSEUM **18** M9

U 3 Volkstheater, Tram 1, 2 Bellaria

1, Burgring 7; tel. 93 45 41-0. Daily except Tuesday 9 a.m.–4 p.m. Admission free from 1 September to 30 April on Saturday, Sunday and holidays.

This building was erected in 1889 as an almost identical counterpart to the slightly older Kunsthistorisches Museum, which it faces across a little park. For a long time the Natural History Museum led a Cinderella existence compared with the art collection, as you can tell by the dilapidated state of the building. However, the museum's financial position has recently improved and renovation work (such as electrification throughout!) has begun.

The museum began with the private collection of Francis Stephan of Lorraine, Maria Theresia's husband (1708–65). Some of the most interesting display items are the skeletons of prehistoric animals, the figurine of the Venus of Willendorf (early Stone Age) and a floral bouquet made of precious stones belonging to Maria Theresia. The museum has excellent facilities for children.

ÖSTERREICHISCHE GALERIE
(See also Modern Art Museums.)

1 MUSEUM MITTELALTERLICHER ÖSTERREICHISCHER KUNST
(UNTERES BELVEDERE)   **19** O8   Tram 71 Marokkanergasse.
3, Rennweg 6a; tel. 78 41 58-0. Daily except Monday 10 a.m.–4 p.m.
The most recent addition to the Austrian Gallery, this museum in the baroque palace of the Lower Belvedere contains Austrian art from the 12th to the 16th centuries, with a distinct emphasis on the 15th century.

2 ÖSTERREICHISCHES   Tram 71 Marokkanergasse
BAROCKMUSEUM (UNTERES BELVEDERE)   **19** O8
3, Rennweg 6a; tel. 78 41 58-0. Daily except Monday 10 a.m.–4 p.m..
This original collection of the Österreichische Galerie houses late-17th- and 18th-century Austrian art, both secular and religious.

ÖSTERREICHISCHES MUSEUM   U 3 Stubentor
FÜR ANGEWANDTE KUNST   **19** O9
1, Stubenring 5; tel. 71 136-0. Tuesday, Wednesday, Friday 10 a.m.– 4 p.m., Thursday 10 a.m.–6 p.m., Sunday 10 a.m.–1 p.m.
Built to house the Museum of Art and Industry (founded in 1864), the connection between the two is shown in the decoration of the building. It was designed between 1868 and 1871 by Heinrich von Ferstel in the style of neo-Florentine Renaissance and is the oldest museum of its kind in Europe. There are collections of Far Eastern art, Islamic art, glass and ceramics, book illustration and bookbinding, metalwork, furniture and woodwork, textiles and carpets, and photography.

45

ÖSTERREICHISCHES   U 1, U 3 Stephansplatz
THEATERMUSEUM   **19** N9
(Formerly Österreichisches Theatermuseum and Theatersammlung der Österreichischen Nationalbibliothek).
1, Lobkowitzplatz 2; tel. 512 88 00-0. Daily except Monday 10 a.m.– 5 p.m.
In 1991, the two collections were merged and moved to more adequate quarters in the Palais Lobkowitz, an interesting building in its own right built in 1687. The theatre collection of the Austrian National Library had been founded in 1922 on the acquisition of the personal collection of Hugo Thiemig and since then it has steadily expanded to include one million items. The Austrian theatre museum, founded in 1975 to display the collection to the public, consisted mainly of costumes and stage models from the past 200 years, many of which will now be put on display. Twice a year the museum stages small specialized exhibitions

Downstairs, there is a children's section of the theatre museum, which opens daily at 11 a.m. and 3 p.m. for a short time, but also by prior arrangement.

Memorial rooms to various famous actors, playwrights and composers are still at the old address of the museum at 1, Hanusch-gasse 3; tel. 512 24 27. U 1, U 2, U 4 Karlsplatz.

MODERN ART MUSEUMS

MUSEUM MODERNER KUNST

1 MUSEUM MODERNER KUNST:　　🚌 13A, Tram D Südbahnhof
MUSEUM DES 20. JAHRHUNDERTS　25 O6

3, Schweizergarten; tel. 78 25 50. Daily except Wednesday 10 a.m.–7 p.m. Closed 1 January, Good Friday, Easter Sunday, 1 May, Corpus Christi, 1–2 November, 24–25 December.

This museum, a former world exhibition pavilion for the Brussels EXPO in 1960, lovingly called *20er–Haus* ('Twenties House') by the Viennese, contains no permanent exhibition apart from a 'Garden of Sculptures', but holds various exhibitions on a wide variety of 20th-century art.

2 MUSEUM MODERNER KUNST:　　🚌 40 A Bauernfeldplatz,
PALAIS LIECHTENSTEIN　12 M11　　Tram D Fürstengasse

9, Fürstengasse 1; tel. 34 12 59. Daily except Tuesday 10 a.m.–7 p.m. Closed 1 January, Good Friday, Easter Sunday, 1 May, Corpus Christi, 1–2 November, 24–25 December.

Based on the Ludwig collection, this fine baroque mansion houses a permanent exhibition of international and Austrian 20th-century art and is probably the best place to study trends in post-war Austrian art, such as abstract art and fantastic realism.

OSTERREICHISCHE GALERIE
(See also HISTORICAL AND ART MUSEUMS.)

1 ÖSTERREICHISCHE GALERIE DES 19.　Tram D Belvederegasse
UND 20. JAHRHUNDERTS (OBERES BELVEDERE)　25 O7

3, Prinz-Eugen-Straße 27; tel. 78 41 58-0. Daily except Monday 10 a.m.–4 p.m.

The part of the Österreichische Galerie on show in the Upper Palace of the Belvedere is the collection of 19th- and 20th-century Austrian art, the most representative collection of *fin de siècle* art in Vienna. So for all those who have wondered about the relative dearth of Klimt and Schiele in other museums, this is where to look for them. One of the most stunning small galleries in Europe.

2 NEUE GALERIE IN DER STALLBURG   19 N9   U 3 Herrengasse
1, Reitschulgasse 2; tel. 533 60 45. Tuesday, Wednesday, Thursday 10 a.m.–4 p.m., Saturday and Sunday 9 a.m.–4 p.m. Closed Monday and Friday.
An international collection of 19th- and 20th-century paintings that used to be in the gallery of the Kunstgeschichtliches Museum. Also some sculptures from the same period.

THEMATIC AND SCIENTIFIC MUSEUMS

GLOCKENMUSEUM   Tram O Troststraße
(GLOCKENSAMMLUNG PFUNDNER)
10, Troststraße 38; tel. 64 34 60. Wednesday 2–5 p.m.
The Bell Museum houses a private collection of more than 80 church bells and documents the history and process of bell founding.

47

HEERESGESCHICHTLICHES   12 🚆 69 A Ghegastraße
MUSEUM   25 P6
3, Ghegastraße, Arsenal Objekt 1; tel. 78 23 03-0. Daily except Friday 10 a.m.–4 p.m. Closed 1 January, Easter Sunday, 1 May, Whitsun, Corpus Christi, 1–2 November, 24–25 December.
This museum documents the military history of Austria from the Thirty Years' War to, tellingly, the beginning of the 20th century. The First World War is only inadequately presented, and there is very little from after that time, but a whole room is given over to the assassination of Archduke Franz Ferdinand in 1914 (including the car and the blood-stained uniform). The museum gives a very good documentary of the Austro-Hungarian navy, complete with many excellent models of ships.

MUSEUM FÜR   Tram 1, 2 Babenbergerstraße
VÖLKERKUNDE   18 M9
1, Neue Burg (Heldenplatz/Burgring); tel. 587 62 11-0. Monday, Thursday, Friday, Saturday 10 a.m.–13 p.m., Wednesday 10 a.m.–5 p.m., Sunday 9 a.m.–1 p.m. Closed Tuesday.

Based on the collections of the former ethnological department of the Kunsthistorisches Museum, this was established as an independent research institution in 1928. The galleries have a quaint look about them, but they contain extremely interesting collections – a major collection of early Mexican treasures; the most comprehensive collection and documentation on the medieval west African Benin culture anywhere; James Cook's Hawaii collection – as well as the many rare objects assembled by the Austrian research expeditions of the last century. The ethnographical museum also organizes important exhibitions in cooperation with foreign collections. Despite the sometimes old-fashioned methods of presentation, this is definitely one of the world's foremost ethnographical museums.

ÖSTERREICHISCHES FILMMUSEUM

1, Augustinerstraße 1; tel. 533 70 54-0.
(See also CINEMA.)

ÖSTERREICHISCHES MUSEUM FÜR VOLKSKUNDE 18 L10

Tram 5 Laudongasse

8, Laudongasse 15–19; tel. 43 89 05-0. Tuesday to Friday 9 a.m.–4 p.m., Saturday, Sunday 9 a.m.–1 p.m. Closed Monday.
The Austrian Museum of Folklore has a collection of items relating to Austrian religious and secular folklore.

ÖSTERREICHISCHES TABAKMUSEUM 18 M8

U 2 Mariahilferstraße

7, Mariahilfer Straße 2; tel. 526 17 16. Tuesday 10 a.m.–7 p.m., Wednesday to Friday 10 a.m.–3 p.m., Saturday, Sunday 9 a.m.–1 p.m. Closed Monday.
A very pretty museum dedicated exclusively to the history of tobacco, smoking and smoking implements, including the history of tobacco production, processing and sale in Austria. The small stage hall incorporated in the museum is frequently used for cultural events, such as poetry readings and chamber music performances, and also for live shows for television.

PATHOLOGISCH-ANATOMISCHES BUNDESMUSEUM 12 L11

Tram 5 Alserstraße

9, Spitalgasse 2. (Narrenturm 'Fools Tower'); tel. 43 86 72. Thursday (except holidays), guided tours only at 8, 9, 10 a.m.
Founded in 1796, the Museum of Pathological Anatomy now houses about 35,000 exhibits illustrating human diseases, with specimens in bot-

tles, bones and moulds. The building was formerly usas the mental aslyum of the hospital, hence the name 'Fools Tower'. Not for the squeamish.

PUPPEN- UND SPIELZEUGMUSEUM 19 N10

U 1, U 3 Stephansplatz

1, Schulhof 4, 2nd floor. Daily except Monday, 9 a.m.–12.15 p.m. and 1–4.30 p.m. Closed 1 January, 1 May, 25 December.

Next door to the Clock Museum (Uhrenmuseum – see below) is the Doll and Toy Museum, which displays the charming private collection of dolls and mechanical and tin toys belonging to V. Sladky and D. Polzer.

TECHNISCHES MUSEUM 22/23 H7

Tram 52, 58 Schloßallee

14, Mariahilfer Straße 212; tel. 89 101-0. Tuesday to Friday and Sunday 9 a.m.–16.00 p.m., Saturday and Holidays 9 a.m.–1 p.m. Closed Monday, 1 January, Good Friday, 1 May, 1–2 November, 24–25 December.

The Technical Museum for Trade and Industry is the most old-fashioned museum in Vienna – one could actually call it a museum of a museum – altho ugh it was only opened in 1908 and is therefore one of Vienna's youngest major museums. Its contents, however, despite their dusty and cramped conditions, never fail to fascinate. It has examples of the earliest technical devices in most fields, ranging from all means of transport to the world's first typewriter. Outside, there are a number of impressive steam engines. For youngsters, the 'hands-on' exhibits may hold a particular attraction.

49

UHRENMUSEUM 19 N10

U 1, U 3 Stephansplatz

1, Schulhof 2; tel. 533 22 65. Daily except Monday 9 a.m.–12.15 p.m. and 1–4.30 p.m. Closed 1 January, 1 May, 25 December. Admission free.

Hidden in a narrow lane behind Am Hof is the Clock Museum. It is housed in the old Obizzi mansion (built in 1690) and contains 3,000 clocks and watches. Many of the clocks are magnificent works of art, some are integrated into paintings, others part of moving landscapes. Some are curious and some are funny.

Watch out when the full hour is reached, you may well need earplugs!

WIENER TRAMWAY-MUSEUM 20 Q8

U 3 Schlachthausgasse

3, Erdbergstraße 109 (Erdberg Tram depot); tel. 587 31 86. Saturday, Sunday and holidays 9 a.m.–4 p.m. (7 May to 2 October only).

The Vienna Tram Museum comprises a nice collection of all those retired trams from the past hundred years, many of which were used right up to the mid-seventies.

Now you can hire them for trips and functions, or go on a sight-seeing tour at the weekends: Saturday 2.30 p.m., Sunday and holidays 10 a.m. (7 May to 30 October only), leaving from the Otto Wagner Pavilion on the Karlsplatz.

ZIRKUSMUSEUM   13 O8   Tram 21, N Karmeliterplatz
2, Karmelitergasse 9; tel. 33 16 11-229. Open Wednesday 5.30–7 p.m., Saturday 2.30–5 p.m., Sunday 10 a.m.–12 noon. Admission free.

The collection started by Heino Seitler in 1935 was given to the city of Vienna in 1968. It contains photos, props, costumes, posters, etc., from the history of the circus in general as well as some Austrian circuses in particular.

FAMOUS PEOPLE

LUDWIG VAN BEETHOVEN (1770–1827)

The Archbishop of Bonn, a Habsburg archduke, sent the teenage prodigy Beethoven to Vienna in 1787 to study under Mozart. However, family circumstances meant that Beethoven returned home and these studies probably never took place. He came back and stayed here, in a great number of houses, until his death.

He loved the countryside around Vienna and the second movement of the *Pastoral Symphony* is said to have been influenced by the birdsong heard on the Wiesental (Meadow Valley) near Heiligenstadt/Grinzing. Much of his time in Vienna was spent in Döbling because of the proximity of the spa waters, which he hoped would alleviate his hearing problems.

BEETHOVEN MEMORIAL ROOM   Tram 37 Pokornygasse
IN THE EROICA HOUSE   6 L/M13
19, Döblinger Hauptstraße 92; tel. 369 14 24. Daily except Monday 10 a.m.–12.15 p.m. and 1–4.30 p.m.

BEETHOVEN'S APARTMENT   18 M8   U 4 Kettenbrückengasse
6, Laimgrubengasse 22; tel. 37 14 085. Visits to be undertaken by prior arrangement only.

SIGMUND FREUD (1856–1939)

Sigmund Freud, the founder of psychoanalysis, was born in Moravia in 1856 of Jewish parents. He became famous for his treatment of neuroses in the 1890s, and was the first to study the role of the subconscious in psychiatric disorders using the technique of free association in place of hypnosis.

He was made a professor at the University of Vienna in 1902. His revolutionary theories and the importance he placed on human sexuality gave him a certain notoriety and led to rifts with many of his colleagues. The influence of his ideas and writings has extended far beyond the disciplines of medicine and psychology.

Freud fled to Hampstead, London in 1938 to escape from the occupying Nazis and continued to practice his theories until he finally became too ill. He died in London on 23 September 1939, in the house that is now the Freud Museum, open to the public. The study where he gave two or three consultations a day has been kept by his daughter Anna exactly as it was when he died.

FREUD'S HOME 12 M10/11   U 2 Schottentor **51**
9, Berggasse 19; tel. 31 15 96. Daily 9 a.m.–3 p.m.

JOSEPH HAYDN (1732–1809)

Although Haydn, the father of the classical symphony and the string quartet, spent the greater part of his life in Eisenstadt, he spent the last years of his life in semi-retirement in Vienna.

A small museum has been established in the house where Haydn lived during his stay in Vienna (1755/6–1809); he also died here.

On hearing of the great composer's death, Napoleon, who was occupying the city for the second time, had a guard of honour put at his house and fired a 21-gun salute at his funeral.

HAYDN MUSEUM 18 K7   Tram 5, 52, 58 Kaiserstraße
6, Haydngasse 9; tel. 596 13 07. Open Tuesday to Sunday 10 a.m.–12.15 p.m. and 1–4.30 p.m. Closed 1 January, 1 May, (Christmas) 25 December.

FRANZ LEHAR (1870–1948) 6 M15   Tram D Nußdorf
19, Hackhofergasse 18 (Lehár-Schlößl, Schikaneder-Schlößl); tel. 37 18 213. Open for groups by prior arrangement.
Mostly famous as a composer of operettas, such as *The Merry Widow*.

WOLFGANG AMADEUS MOZART (1756–1791)

Mozart may have been born in Salzburg, but it was in Vienna that he lived for most of his short life. It seems that there is hardly a palace or house in the inner city that does not lay some claim to the maestro. The following short walk enables you to visit a number of important Mozart sights.

From the Mozart monument in the Burggarten (executed by V. Tilgner in 1896), go to Palais Palffy at Josefsplatz 6, where Mozart performed to a private audience in 1762 and again in 1784. Michaelerplatz was the site (until 1888) of the old Burgtheater, where a number of Mozart's operas were first performed, and two of Mozart's six children were baptized in the Michaelerkirche. Go down Kohlmarkt and Tuchlauben and into Milchgasse, where at No. 1 ('Zum Auge Gottes') Mozart lived in 1781, subsequently marrying Constanze, the daughter of his landlady, Frau Weber.

Not far away, in the square Am Hof, is the Palais Collalto, where Mozart used to give concerts. Down the Heidenschuß and the Tiefer Graben is the house (No. 18) where Mozart and his father lived in the summer of 1773. Climb up the steps Am Gestade, passing the church of Maria am Gestade on your right, and go on to beautiful Judenplatz: Mozart lived at No. 3 from 1783 to 1784, and at No. 4, with Constanze, from 1789 to 1790.

Head back towards the Stephansplatz and go through the archway behind the cathedral into Domgasse to visit the famous Figaro House. This was Mozart's apartment between 1784 and 1787 and is now a museum, displaying original manuscripts and other Mozart memorabilia. Via the picturesque Blutgasse, you reach Singerstraße with the church and the house of the Deutscher Orden at No. 7. Mozart lived here in 1781 when he was in Vienna with his patron, Archbishop Colloredo of Salzburg.

A short walk up Singerstraße brings you to the Stephansdom, where at the Totenkapelle (outside on the north-eastern corner, opposite the opening to Schulerstraße), Mozart's body was consecrated for burial on 6 December 1791.

FRANZ SCHUBERT (1797–1828)

SCHUBERT MUSEUM   Tram D Nußdorf
AT SCHUBERT'S BIRTHPLACE   **12** L11/12
9, Nußdorfer Straße 54; tel. 345 99 24. Daily except Monday 10 a.m.–12.15 p.m. and 1–4.30 p.m.

One of the few great composers actually born in Vienna, Schubert was the musician of the middle classes, not the aristocracy (who revelled in Beethoven). He was a prolific composer but much of his work has been lost due to his lack of organization; he never found real acclaim in his lifetime.

JOHANN STRAUSS THE YOUNGER   U 1 Nestroyplatz
(1825–1899) **13** O/P10
2, Praterstraße 54; tel. 24 01 21. Daily except Monday 10 a.m.–12.15 p.m. and 1–4.30 p.m.
Strauss became a bandleader against the will of his composer father. A talented and productive composer, he specialized in waltzes and later operettas – *Die Fledermaus* (1874) and *The Gypsy Baron* (1885) being among his best known.

OTTO WAGNER (1841–1918)
Otto Wagner was Vienna's most famous architect before the turn of the century. He played a major part in the replanning of Vienna at the end of the 19th century. He designed the Stadtbahn (now called U 6) as well as the regulation of the river Wien. Several of his buildings are listed under ARCHITECTURE (see page 36).

53

HOFPAVILLON OTTO WAGNER **22/23** G/H7   U 4 Hietzing
13, Schönbrunner Schloßstraße; tel. 877 15 71. Daily except Monday 9 a.m.–12.15 p.m. and 1–6 p.m.
A former station building, now mainly interesting for its interior architecture by Otto Wagner and the photographs showing its development and history.

OTTO WAGNER'S   Tram 46, 🚌 13A Strozzigasse
LAST RESIDENCE **18** L9
7, Döblergasse 4; tel. 93 22 33. Monday to Friday 9 a.m.–12 noon (July to September on request).
Otto Wagner's last residence (1912-18) is now an archive concentrating on publications about Otto Wagner (no originals).

OTTO WAGNER PAVILION **18** N8   U1, U2, U4 Karlsplatz
1, Karlsplatz. Daily except Monday 10 a.m.–12.15 and 1–4.30 p.m. (1 April to 31 October only). Closed 1 May.
Formerly part of the Karlsplatz tram station.

Antiquitäten
B. HORN
Einkauf u. Verkauf von Antiquitäten Gold und Silberwaren
Alte Gläser Porzellan
Holzfiguren
Uhren Bronzen

In a city as renowned for art and culture as Vienna, it would be surprising if there were not a multitude of art galleries displaying and selling the latest works by contemporary artists. Many art galleries and antique shops are to be found clustered around the Albertina Art Museum and the Dorotheum, Vienna's main auction house, while still more are tucked away in back courtyards or in the cobbled streets around Bäckerstraße or behind the Stephansdom. As there is so much variety to be found within walking distance in the inner city we have concentrated on this area.

ART GALLERIES

GALERIE AM OPERNRING 18/19 M/N8   U 1, U 2, U 4 Karlsplatz
1, Opernring 17; tel. 587 97 24. Monday to Friday 10 a.m.–1 p.m., 2–6 p.m., Saturday 10 a.m.–1 p.m.
Exhibitions of contemporary artists, especially from Austria and Spain, concentrating on paintings and graphic art.

GALERIE ANGELA 19 N9   U 1, U 3 Stephansplatz
1, Blutgasse 3, 2nd Backyard; tel. 512 81 63.
Beautiful stuff from the 'Neue Wiener Werkstätte' in a lovely setting – worth **55** visiting just for the courtyard with its balconies and trailing ivy.

GALERIE BEI DER ALBERTINA 19 N9   U 1, U 3 Stephansplatz
1, Lobkowitzplatz 1; tel. 513 14 16. Monday to Friday 10 a.m.–4 p.m., Saturday 10 a.m.–1 p.m.
Twentieth-century Austrian art, concentrating on the solid and beautiful, especially art nouveau and early-20th-century 'modern classics'.

GALERIE CHOBOT 19 N9   U 1, U 3 Stephansplatz
1, Domgasse 6; tel. 512 53 32. Tuesday to Friday 1–7 p.m., Saturday 10 a.m.–1 p.m.
This gallery, in an old house with a beautiful courtyard from 1761 (it used to house Vienna's oldest café) specializes in paintings and sculptures by Austrian and European artists after 1945.

Antique shops – with something for everyone – tend to cluster around St Stephan.

GALERIE CONTACT   **19** N9   U 1, U 3 Stephansplatz
1, Singerstraße 17 (Palais Rottal; entry via Grünangergasse); tel. 512 98 80. Tuesday to Friday 11 a.m.–6 p.m., Saturday 10 a.m.–1 p.m.
Offers a cross-section of modern paintings and sculptures.

GALERIE FABER   **19** N9   U 1, U 3 Stephansplatz
1, Köllnerhofgasse 6; tel. 512 24 14. Tuesday to Friday 1–6 p.m., Saturday 10 a.m.–1 p.m.
A photogallery, showing both contemporary and historical work, even in thematic shows, but its main interest is in contemporary Austrian art.

GALERIE HEIKE CURTZE   **19** N9   U 1, U 3 Stephansplatz
1, Seilerstätte 15; tel. 512 93 75. Tuesday to Friday 3–7 p.m., Saturday 11 a.m.–2 p.m.
Contemporary Austrian artists, specializing in the not-so-young and not-so-cheap, e.g. Rainer, Nitsch, Attersee.

GALERIE HOFSTÄTTER   U 1, U 3 Stephansplatz
1, Bräunerstrasse 7; tel. 512 32 55. Monday to Friday 10 a.m.–6.p.m., Saturday 10 a.m.–12.30 p.m.
Genuine Art Nouveau and Art Deco jewellery, modern and contemporary Austrian art in one of Vienna's most beautiful galleries.

GALERIE INTAKT   **19** N10/O9   U 1, U 3 Stephansplatz
1, Fleischmarkt 11; tel. 533 20 374. Tuesday to Friday 4–7 p.m.
This is a gallery run by the 'Aktionsgemeinschaft bildender Künstlerinnen' showing art by contemporary female artists.

GALERIE NÄCHST ST STEPHAN   **19** N9   U 1, U 3 Stephansplatz
1, Grünangergasse 1; tel. 512 12 66. Tuesday to Friday 10 a.m.–6 p.m., Saturday 11 a.m.–2 p.m.
Predominantly international and Austrian avant-garde.

GALERIE SONNENFELS   **19** N/O9   U 1, U 4 Schwedenplatz
1, Sonnenfelsgasse 11; tel. 513 39 19. Monday to Friday 2 –6 p.m., Saturday 10 a.m.–1 p.m.
Interesting gallery offering primitive African art.

GALERIE V & V   **18** L8   🚌 13A, Tram 52, 58 Kirchengasse
7, Lindengasse 5; tel. 93 12 07. Monday to Friday 11 a.m.–7 p.m., Saturday 11 a.m.–2 p.m.
Contemporary jewellery by international and Austrian artists.

GLASGALERIE KLUTE   **18** L8   U 1, U 3 Stephansplatz
1, Franziskanerplatz 6 (Leherb-Haus); tel. 513 53 22. Monday to Friday 11 a.m.–6 p.m., Saturday 10 a.m.–12 noon.
Modern glass sculptures by international artists; new exhibitions every two months. Furniture and lamps in glass and steel.

KUNSTBÜRO WIEN   **19** N9/10   U 1, U 3 Stephansplatz
1, Bauernmarkt 9; tel. 533 72 22. Monday to Friday 1–6 p.m., Saturday 10 a.m.–1 p.m.
Austrian and international contemporary artists. Mainly sculpture, but also paintings.

REM   **19** N7   U 1 Taubstummengasse
4, Mozartplatz 4/2; tel. 65 28 89. Tuesday to Friday 3–7 p.m.
Gallery run by contemporary Austrian artists selling their own innovative products.

ANTIQUES

Vienna has many antique shops of all kinds, especially in the Dorotheergasse, Stallburggasse and Spiegelgasse area of the First District. But if you are on the hunt for antiques your first stop should be the Dorotheum, Vienna's state-run auction house and pawnbroker. **57**

  The quality of the items on sale varies enormously and it is worth repeated visits. It is interesting even if you are not looking for anything in particular.

DOROTHEUM   **19** N9   U 1, U 3 Stephansplatz
1, Dorotheergasse 11; tel. 515 60-0. Art auctions every Thursday at 2.30 p.m., objects on exhibition one week beforehand (Monday to Friday 10 a.m.–6 p.m.).
The Dorotheum is the state's auction house and has a number of branches all over Vienna, dealing in all sorts of antiques and other objects. Worthwhile art auctions are held only at Dorotheergasse.

ANTIK KELLER   **18** M10   U 2 Schottentor
1, Liebiggasse 4; tel. 43 07 19. Monday to Friday 10 a.m.–6 p.m., Saturday 10 a.m.–12 p.m.
Informal. Furniture and lamps mainly. University surroundings keep prices reasonable.

ANTIQUITÄTEN R. JANKOVIC   **19** N9   U 1, U 3 Stephansplatz
1, Spiegelgasse 21; tel. 513 87 59. Monday to Friday 9 a.m.–6 p.m., Saturday 9 a.m.–12 p.m.
All sorts of pictures and paintings.

ANTIQUITÄTEN E. U. J. STÖHR   **19** N9   U 1, U 3 Stephansplatz
1, Stallburggasse 2; tel. 512 89 73. Monday to Friday 10 a.m.–1 p.m., 3–6 p.m., Saturday 10 a.m.–1 p.m.
Vintage jewellery and decorations.

ANTIQUITÄTEN WORATSCH   **19** M10   U 1, U 3 Stephansplatz
1, Wipplingerstraße 20; tel. 533 52 54. Monday to Friday 10 a.m.–12.30 p.m., 3–6 p.m.
Furniture, arts and crafts from the 19th century, specializing in Biedermeier.

C. BEDNARCZYK   **19** N9   U 1, U 3 Stephansplatz
1, Dorotheergasse 12; tel. 512 44 45. Monday to Friday 12 noon–6 p.m., Saturday 10 a.m.–1 p.m.
Pictures, glass, porcelain, silver and 18th-century French furniture.

58 **GUY FARRON**   **19** N9   U 1, U 3 Stephansplatz
1, Spiegelgasse 8; tel. 512 87 66. Monday to Friday 10.30 a.m.–1 p.m., 3–6 p.m., Saturday 10 a.m.–12 noon.
Predominantly furniture from the 17th to the 19th century, but also old Dutch paintings and archaeological finds.

FOTO-ANTIQUARIAT   U 1, U 3 Stephansplatz
H. SEEMANN   **19** N9
1, Seilergasse 19; tel. 513 64 91. Monday to Friday 10.30 a.m.–1.30 p.m. and 3.30–6 p.m.
Photos, pictures and postcards only.

GALERIE ZACKE   **19** N/O9   U 1, U 3 Stephansplatz
1, Schulerstraße 15; tel. 512 22 23. Monday to Friday 10 a.m.–6 p.m., Saturday 10 a.m.–1 p.m.
Antique art from Asia spanning the past 4,000 years.

C. & G. JUNKER   **12** M12   Tram 37, 38,
      40A Nußdorferstraße/Alserbachstraße
9, Liechtenstein Straße 104; tel. 310 88 02. Monday to Friday 10 a.m.–6 p.m., Saturday 9.30 a.m.–12.30 p.m.

A spacious showroom stuffed with lovely Biedermeier furniture; they also have a shop near the Dorotheum.

KABUL SHOP **18** M9   U 3 Herrengasse
1, Herrengasse 6–8; tel. 535 34 80. Monday to Friday 9 a.m.–6 p.m., Saturday 9 a.m.–12 noon

Rugs, textiles and antiques from the Middle East, a veritable Ali Baba's cave. They also do some lovely heavy bedouin jewellery.

KONRAD'S ALTER SCHMUCK **11** K10   Tram 40, 41 Aumannplatz
18, Währinger Straße 155; tel. 47 77 17. Monday to Friday 10 a.m.–6 p.m., Saturday 9 a.m.–12 noon.

Antique jewellery and decorations, beginning in the Biedermeier period. Own workshop for repairs of antique jewellery.

KUNSTHANDEL   U 1 Taubstummengasse
STEPHAN ANDRÉEWITCH **25** N7
4, Favoritenstraße 10; tel. 505 99 73. Monday to Friday 9 a.m.–6 p.m., Saturday 9 a.m.–12 noon.

Pictures and furniture.

THONET **19** N9   U 1, U 3 Stephansplatz **59**
1, Kohlmarkt 6; tel. 533 77 88. Monday to Friday 9 a.m.-6 p.m., Thursday 9 a.m.–8 p.m., Saturday 9 a.m.–12 .30 p.m.

Furniture makers producing high-quality individual pieces to order. They have been in the business for a long time and their products are now much prized by collectors.

WIENER INTERIEUR **19** N9   U 1, U 3 Stephansplatz
1, Dorotheergasse 14; tel. 512 28 98. Monday to Friday 10 a.m.–6 p.m., Saturday 10 a.m.–1 p.m.

A tiny boutique ingeniously maintaining a carefully designed uncluttered look. They have a good line in *Jugendstil* and art deco vases and jewellery.

WIENER KUNSTSTÄTTE –   U 1, U 3 Stephansplatz
ANTIQUITÄTEN BEIM PALAIS FERSTEL **18** M9/10
1, Strauchgasse 2; tel. 535 42 77. Monday to Friday 10 a.m.–6 p.m., Saturday 10 a.m.–1 p.m.

Wide collection of art nouveau paintings, furniture and objects.

Because of the way Vienna has developed – a centre surrounded by many small adjoining villages – the style of shopping is a little different from that of other capital cities. People tend to shop in their local area for their everyday needs, but for special items they will usually head for the First District as it offers by far the most exciting possibilities. For the visitor, it is worthwhile spending a little time exploring, hunting out those hidden corners that may conceal a little shopper's paradise, though not very often a bargain.

Credit cards are not commonly used in Austria – no food shops (apart from large Julius Meindl supermarkets) take them and cash is preferred elsewhere too.

TAX-FREE SHOPPING

Many shops are able to arrange tax-free shopping for those not living in Austria. These shops normally advertise the fact with a sticker in the window. It is not difficult to arrange and you can save 13% (VAT) on anything over 1,000 ÖS. Ask the shop to help you.

DUTY-FREE SHOPPING

Here again some refund is given on purchases made in the airport boutiques, provided that the total is above 1,000 ÖS. The all-important figure of 1,000 ÖS can be reached by totalling purchases from different boutiques in the airport, though this may be difficult to arrange.

SHOPPING TIMES

Shops open any time between 6 a.m. and 10 a.m., depending on what they are selling. Many close at lunchtime from 12 noon or 12.30 p.m. until 2 or 3 p.m., except in the First District and most close for the day at 6 p.m., although some supermarkets stay open till 6.30 or 7 p.m., sometimes even a little later. In the First District only, late-night shopping has recently been introduced – the majority of shops in and around the main shopping area now stay open until 8 p.m. on Thursday nights. What you must remember is that on Saturday they all shut promptly between 12 noon and 1 p.m., and remain closed until Monday, so be careful not to get caught without food for the weekend! On the first Saturday of the

Like everything in Vienna, shopping is also an agreeable experience.

month, however, *non-food* shops remain open all day, generally closing at 5 p.m., this is known as *Langer Samstag* or long Saturday. The only things that you can almost always buy, even on a Sunday, are cakes and chocolates in the Konditorei and cafés that remain open to satisfy the Viennese taste for coffee and cakes. There are plans to relax the Austrian laws concerning opening times in the near future, so the times given here may soon change.

CLOTHING

1, JUDENGASSE **19** N10   U 1, U 4 Schwedenplatz
This little street between Schwedenplatz and Judengasse is lined with small boutiques selling highly fashionable clothes; there is also a secondhand shop that usually has some quite worthwhile things in it and further on down the street are some bars and restaurants.

ADONIS **19** N9   U 1, U 3 Stephansplatz
1, Kohlmarkt 11; tel. 533 70 35. Monday to Friday 9 a.m.–6 p.m., Saturday 9 a.m.–1 p.m.
Mildly fashionable men's clothes with some designer labels. Work and leisure clothing with a young feel.

62 ALEXANDER **19** N9   U 1, U 3 Stephansplatz
1, Rauhensteingasse 10; tel. 512 39 46. Monday to Friday 9.30 a.m.–6 p.m., except Thursday 9.30 a.m.–8 p.m., Saturday 9.15 a.m.–12.45 p.m.
For that transcontinental studied casual look. Great products don't come cheap, as Alexander's shows.

E. BRAUN & CO **19** N9   U 1, U 3 Stephansplatz
1, Graben 3; tel. 512 55 05. Monday to Friday 9.15 a.m.–6 p.m., Saturday 9.15 a.m.–1 p.m.
Men's and women's clothes, conventional but certainly not lacking in class. Braun is striking for its old-fashioned, grand emporium style, all it lacks is a liveried porter. Also known for its bed and table linens.

CASETTA **19** N9   U 3 Landstraße Wien Mitte
3, Landstraßer Hauptstraße 1B; tel. 713 51 18. Monday to Friday 9 a.m.–6 p.m., Saturday 9 a.m.–12 noon.
Fashionable boutique selling anything from leggings to suits for the woman about town.

CHANEL BOUTIQUE; W & A JONA **19** N9   U 1, U 3 Stephansplatz
*1, Trattnerhof 1; tel. 533 99 08. Monday to Friday 9.30 a.m.–6 p.m.,
except Thursday 9.30 a.m.–8 p.m., Saturday 10 a.m.–1 p.m., except
Langer Samstag.*
The sort of boutique where one hardly dares raise one's voice above a
whisper – an appropriate outlet for the most hallowed of daywear designers.

CHEGINI **19** N9   U 1, U 3 Stephansplatz
*1, Kohlmarkt 7; tel. 535 27 52. Monday to Friday 9.45 a.m.–6 p.m.,
except Thursday 9.45 a.m.–8 p.m., Saturday 10 a.m.–1 p.m.*
A really thrilling selection of those designers we all know, or would like
to get to know.

DAMART **19** N9   U 1, U 4 Schwedenplatz
*1, Lichtensteg 3; tel. 533 03 59. Monday to Friday 9 a.m.–6 p.m.,
Saturday 9 a.m.–12 noon.*
Invaluable source of warm clothing for Austria's bitterly cold winters.

DANTENDORFER **19** N9   U 1, U 3 Stephansplatz
*1, Weihburggasse 9; tel. 512 59 65. Monday to Friday 10 a.m.–6 p.m.,
Saturday 9.30 a.m.–12.30 p.m.*
A sample of what designers have to offer in a casual vein.

DA WEISS **19** N9   U 1, U 4 Schwedenplatz
*1, Landskrongasse 8; tel. 533 53 34. Monday to Friday 10 a.m.–6 p.m.,
Saturday 9.30 a.m.–1 p.m.*
Offers some amusing punk cum sixties-revival fashion.

63

DOMANI **19** N9   U 1, U 3 Stephansplatz
*1, Rotenturmstraße 14; tel. 512 13 60. Monday to Friday 9 a.m.–6 p.m.,
Saturday 9.30 a.m.–12.30 p.m.*
Selling, among many other things, Moschino accessories.

BOUTIQUE ERIKA EISENBAUL **19** N9   U 1, U 3 Stephansplatz
*1, Plankengasse 4; tel. 512 28 91. Monday to Friday 10 a.m.–
6 p.m.,Saturday 9 a.m.–1 p.m.*
Most notable for the Kenzo she sells.

ETOILE **19** N9   U 1, U 4 Schwedenplatz
*1, Lugeck 3; tel. 512 62 70. Monday to Friday 9.30 a.m.–6 p.m., Saturday
9.30 a.m.–1 p.m.*
For women, a small, but exclusive, boutique with a powerful stock of classic designs including Armani, Kenzo, Robert Clergerie, etc.

FEELING BLUE   19 N9 $\qquad$ U 1, U 4 Schwedenplatz
1, Bäckerstraße 2; tel. 513 59 23.
Another in a series of boutiques catering to the passing university traffic. This one is an excellent source of blue denim, or for that matter black,
white, red, etc.

FIDSCHI'S   19 N9 $\qquad$ U 1, U 4 Schwedenplatz
1, Wollzeile 5; tel. 512 39 63. Monday to Friday 9.30 a.m.–7.30 p.m.,
except Thursday 9.30 a.m.–9 p.m., Saturday 9.30 a.m.–5 p.m.
One of several shops in this passage between Bäckerstraße and
Wollzeile, Fidschi's concentrates on very casual everyday fashion with
a smattering of designer names – Katharine Hamnett is one.

FULL POWER   19 N9 $\qquad$ U 1, U 3 Stephansplatz
1, Trattnerhof 1; tel. 587 71 10, and 6, Mariahilfer Straße 77 & 103; tel.
586 02 35. Monday to Friday 10 a.m.–6.30 p.m., except Thursday 10
a.m.–8 p.m., Saturday 9 a.m.–1 p.m.
This looks like the sort of dive that should have been in Carnaby Street
30 years ago, and sells the clothes to match.

GUYS & DOLLS   19 N10 $\qquad$ U 1, U 4 Schwedenplatz
1, Schultergasse 2 (off Tuchlauben); tel. 535 42 83. Monday to Friday
10 a.m.–6 p.m., Saturday 9.30 a.m.–12.30 p.m.
64 It describes itself inappropriately as 'Basic & Extravagant'. Some witty
ideas should reward a search through the rails.

HANDSCHUH PETER   12 L11 $\qquad$ U 6 Währinger Straße/Volksoper
18, Währinger Straße 89; tel. 42 35 26. Monday to Friday 8 a.m.–5 p.m.,
closed Saturday.
Gloves of every size, shape and quality.

HOUSE OF GENTLEMAN   19 N9 $\qquad$ U 1, U 3 Stephansplatz
1, Kohlmarkt 12; tel. 533 32 58. Monday to Friday 9 a.m.–6 p.m., Saturday
9 a.m.–1 p.m.
Traditional men's outfitters with some women's classics too.

KALI   19 N10 $\qquad$ U 1, U 3 Stephansplatz
1, Bauernmarkt 12; tel. 533 62 21. Monday to Friday 10 a.m.–6 p.m.,
Saturday 9.30 a.m.–12.30 p.m.
A really unusual style of dressing is possible with the help of this delightful
boutique. They also sell some Stéphane Kelian shoes.

KNIZE   19 N9   U 1, U 3 Stephansplatz
1, Graben 13; tel. 512 21 19. Monday to Friday 9.30 a.m.–6 p.m., except Thursday 9.30 a.m.–8 p.m., Saturday 9.30 a.m.–12.30 p.m.
Custom-made, classic men's clothes and about as exclusive as you can get. Shop interior designed by the well-known Secessionist architect Adolf Loos.

LADY ANTHONY   19 N9   U 1, U 3 Stephansplatz
1, Kärntner Straße 53; tel. 512 41 55. Monday to Friday 9.30 a.m.–6 p.m., Saturday 9.30 a.m.–1 p.m.
The female counterpart to Sir Anthony.

LESCHKA, P.C. & CO.   19 N9   U 1, U 3 Stephansplatz
1, Graben 16; tel. 533 60 68, 535 01 27. Monday to Friday 9 a.m.–6 p.m., except Thursday 9 a.m.–8 p.m., Saturday 9 a.m.–12.30 p.m.
A particularly good source of jumpers and cardigans.

MYLS   19 N9   U 1, U 4 Schwedenplatz
1, Köllnerhofgasse 2; tel. 513 80 17. Monday to Friday 10.30 a.m.–6 p.m., Saturday 10.30 a.m.–1 p.m.
Here they sell Body Map – a young English design group – and some Viennese designers in the same high-fashion vein.

PER LA DONNA   19 N10   U 1, U 4 Schwedenplatz
1, Judenplatz 5; tel. 533 73 54. Monday to Friday 9.30 a.m.–6 p.m., Saturday 9.30 a.m.–12.30 p.m.
A whole shop full of La Perla, Versace and other designers' underwear.

65

POLO RALPH LAUREN   19 N10   U 4 Kettenbrückengasse
5, Rechte Wienzeile 93.
An inimitable style of his own distinguishes this most American of designers.

PULLOVERIA   19 N9   U 3 Herrengasse
1, Naglergasse 1; tel. 533 68 96/63 85 52. Monday to Friday 9 a.m.–6 p.m., Saturday 9 a.m.–12.30 p.m. Also at 1, Köllnerhofgasse 2; tel. 513 80 57. Monday to Friday 10 a.m.–6 p.m., Saturday 10 a.m.–12.30 p.m.
This has an undeniably Italian look to it, and it may not surprise you that they concentrate on pullovers. They also have shirts and T-shirts in the summer, and a good selection of jackets – including some in leather – parkas and duffel coats.

RESI HAMMERER **19** N9 U 1, U 3 Stephansplatz
1, Kärntner Straße 29-31; tel. 512 69 52. Monday to Friday 9.30 a.m.–6 p.m., except Thursday 9.30 a.m.–8 p.m., Saturday 9.30 a.m.–1 p.m.
Chic in the 'Burberry' tradition is on offer here, with a certain amount of traditional dress as well.

RISMAS & KRASS **19** N10 U 1, U 3 Stephansplatz
1, Marc-Aurel-Straße 4; tel. 533 58 93. Monday to Friday 10 a.m.–6 p.m., Saturday 10 a.m.–12.30 p.m.
A way-out selection of the very latest fashion on offer in Vienna.

SIR ANTHONY **19** N9 U 1, U 3 Stephansplatz.
1, Kärntner Straße 21–23; tel. 512 68 35. Monday to Friday 9 a.m.–6 p.m., Saturday 9 a.m.–1 p.m.
Offers a selection of classics such as Aquascutum, Burberry, Daks, Chester Barrie, D'Avenza, Christian Dior, etc, but is actually more fashion conscious than one might expect. They advertise tax-free shopping facilities and the acceptance of credit cards.

SKAF **19** N9 U 1, U 3 Stephansplatz
1, Jasomirgottstraße 2; tel. 533 04 04, and 1, Singerstraße 27; tel. 512 42 03. Monday to Friday 9.30 a.m.–6.30 p.m., Saturday 9.30 a.m.–1 p.m.
Here is the full design package: shop, clothing and accessories. Names include Joseph and Katharine Hamnett.

66

SYBARIS **18** M9/10 U 3 Herrengasse
1, Herrengasse 17; tel. 535 99 05. Monday to Friday 9 a.m.–6 p.m., Saturday 9 a.m.–12.30 p.m.
For the fashion-conscious young professional when fashion must take a low-profile. There are also children's clothes in the Freyung Passage.

SZENKOVITS **19** N9 U 3 Herrengasse
1, Habsburgergasse 6; tel: 533 70 84. Monday to Friday 9.30 a.m.–6 p.m., except Thursday 9.30 a.m.–8 p.m., Saturday 9.30 a.m.–1 p.m.
An impressive list of designers display their wares here – Polo Ralph Lauren, Cerruti, Moschino among them – with chic for men and women.

TOP SHOP **19** N9 U 1, U 3 Stephansplatz
1, Weihburggasse 7; tel. 512 53 65. Monday to Friday 10 a.m.–6 p.m., Saturday 10 a.m.–12.30 p.m.
This little boutique has an amusing line in interior design – all fixtures and fittings are on wheels. Designers include Norma Kamali and Moschino.

CHAIN STORES

BLAUMAX **19** N10/O9   U 1, U 4 Schwedenplatz
1, Fleischmarkt 20–22; tel. 513 45 31, and many branches.
Jeans chain.

BRIEFTAUBE **19** N9   U 1, U 3 Stephansplatz
1, Graben 11; tel. 512 51 29, and branches.
Attractive casual clothing for women.

DON GIL **19** N9   U 1, U 3 Stephansplatz
1, Kärntner Straße 14; tel. 512 95 23, and branches.
A chain carrying a broad range of men's clothes, lots of designer names
from the sporty to the formal.

FÜRNKRANZ **19** N9   U 1, U 3 Stephansplatz
1, Kärntner Straße 39; tel. 45 85 15, and branches.
The biggest branch of this chain, which offers a good selection of
women's clothes for the sharp dresser. Also offers couture designs.

GAZELLE   *Branches on most shopping streets*
Lingerie of all sorts – all the brands you know from elsewhere and some
that you may not know. You would not have thought there was enough
of a market in Austria for two huge chains selling only underwear, and
might wonder what the Viennese ladies do with theirs, but Gazelle has
a major competitor – Palmers, see below.

67

NAF NAF **12** K12   U 6 Währinger Straße/Volksoper
18, Währinger Straße 106; tel. 310 68 55. Also at 19, Billroth Straße 54;
tel. 42 36 67 32 (Tram 38 Hardtgasse), *and 3, in the Galleria, Landstraßer*
Hauptstraße 97–101; tel. 712 04 32 (U 3, U 4 Landstraße/ Wien Mitte).
These are only some of the outlets for this French group's young-fash-
ion products, which seem to be so popular with Vienna's teenagers. They
offer a line of fun, highly coloured, casual wear, as an alternative to the
ubiquitous American jeans and baseball look.

PALMERS   *Branches on most major shopping streets*
Sells only its own brand of high-quality underwear for men and women
at inflated prices. It is the great competitor to Gazelle and is also well
represented. Its advertising campaigns have frequently got moralists'
knickers in a twist.

TRACHT AND *JAGD* (AUSTRIAN NATIONAL COSTUME, AND HUNTING AND COUNTRY-STYLE CLOTHES)

Tracht is what Austrian traditional clothes are called. They tend to be made of more solid fabrics, with horn buttons, in tones of green and brown, with some embroidery; but today these materials are used in combination with modern fabrics and colours, resulting in a uniquely Austrian country style, which can nevertheless be worn by everybody and everywhere. The female national costume, the *Dirndl*, can range from folksy to formal. Classic items for both sexes are the Loden coat and the *Walkjanker*, both very sturdy but timelessly handsome outdoor gear. Teenage connoisseurs will prefer to look for a Trachten jacket at the weekly fleamarket at the Naschmarkt. Very chic with jeans!

COLLINS   19 N8   U 1, U 2, U 4 Karlsplatz
1, Opernpassage 12; tel. 587 13 05. 1, Opernring Nr. 1; tel. 587 05 40. Monday to Friday 9 a.m.–6 p.m., Saturday 9 a.m.–1 p.m.
Specializes in hats, but also does men's outdoor *Tracht* and women's *Tracht* with a fashionable edge.

HELFORD JERSEY   19 N/O 10   U 1, U 4 Schwedenplatz
1, Franz-Josefs-Kai 19; tel. 533 29 7. Monday to Friday 9 a.m.–6 p.m., Saturday 9 a.m.–12 noon.
It would be hard to find a more unlikely looking shop. The window display features rolls of fabric that might have been there for 20 years. Inside, the selection becomes even more improbable: Tyrolean *Walkjanker*, a mixture of baseball caps, and more fabrics. The walker jackets are better value here than elsewhere.

LANZ   19 N9   U 1, U 3 Stephansplatz
1, Kärntner Straße 10; tel. 512 24 56. Monday to Friday 9 a.m.–6 p.m., except Thursday 9 a.m.–8 p.m., Saturday 9 a.m.–1 p.m.
One of the best shops for traditional Austrian clothing with a specially good selection for outdoors.

LODEN PLANKL   18/9 M/N9   U 3 Herrengasse1
1, Michaelerplatz 6; tel. 533 80 32. Monday to Friday 9 a.m.–6 p.m., Saturday 9 a.m.–1 p.m.
A really excellent source of Austrian traditional clothing with genuine style.

TRACHTEN TOSTMANN **18** M10 U 2 Schottentor
1, Schottengasse 3a; tel. 533 53 31. Monday to Friday 9 a.m.–6.30 p.m., Saturday 9 a.m.–12.30 p.m.
Until you have been to Tostmann, you haven't really seen Tracht. The children's department is full of the prettiest *Dirndln*, knitted jackets and lovely loden capes, and the men's and women's departments do not lag far behind. There is also a charming gift shop.

TURCZYNSKI **19** N/O9 U 3 Stubentor
1, Wollzeile 18; tel. 512 82 24. Monday to Friday 9 a.m.–6 p.m., Saturday 9 a.m.–12 noon.
Traditional Austrian country and sporting clothes for men.

WITZKY **19** N9 U 1, U 3 Stephansplatz
1, Stephansplatz 7; tel. 512 48 43. Monday to Friday 10 a.m.–6 p.m., Saturday 10 a.m.–12.30 p.m.
A more fashion-conscious or urbane look at the traditional dress styles.

SHOES AND LEATHER GOODS

ALTA MODA **19** N9 U 1, U 3 Stephansplatz
1, Seilergasse 14; tel. 512 49 61. Monday to Friday 9 a.m.–6 p.m., Saturday 9 a.m.–12.30 p.m.
Also at 6, Mariahilfer Straße 71; tel. 586 23 26. Monday to Friday 9 a.m.–6 p.m., Saturday 9 a.m.–12.30 p.m.
Italian bags and haute couture shoes.

69

ANTONELLA **19** N9 U 1, U 3 Stephansplatz
1, Führichgasse 4; tel. 512 41 73. Monday to Friday 9.30 a.m.–6 p.m., Saturday 9.30 a.m.–12.30 p.m.
What a find this shop is! A tiny, cluttered boutique with plenty of racks of shoes packing in the best names in shoe design at unusually reasonable prices.

BALLY **19** N9 U 1, U 3 Stephansplatz
1, Kärntner Straße 9; tel. 512 14 61, and many branches. Monday to Friday 9 a.m.–6 p.m., except Thursday 9 a.m.–8 p.m., Saturday 9 a.m.–1 p.m.
This ubiquitous shop is well represented in Vienna, selling its range of elegant Swiss shoes and bags.

BOTTEGA VENETA   **19** N9   U 1, U 3 Stephansplatz
1, Stock-im-Eisen-Platz 3; tel. 512 99 72. Monday to Friday 9.30 a.m.–6 p.m., except Thursday 9.30 a.m.–8 p.m., Saturday 9 a.m.–1 p.m.
Range of fashionable shoes.

BRUNO MAGLI   **19** N9   U 1, U 3 Stephansplatz
1, Stephansplatz 4; tel. 512 24 02. Monday to Friday 9.30 a.m.–6 p.m., Saturday 9.30 a.m.–1 p.m.
Classic men's and women's shoes.

DA GIOVANNI   **19** N9   U 1, U 4 Schwedenplatz
1, Lugeck 7; tel. 512 42 40. Monday to Friday 9.45 a.m.–6 p.m., Saturday 9.30 a.m.–12.30 p.m.
A wide range of smart shoes for men and women.

DE LA RUE   **19** N9   U 1, U 3 Stephansplatz
1, Seilergasse 3; tel. 512 82 79. Monday to Friday 9 a.m.–6 p.m., Saturday 9 a.m.–1 p.m.
Also at 1, Hotel Marriott, Parkring 12a; tel. 513 20 29.. Monday to Friday 9 a.m.–6 p.m., Saturday 9 a.m.–1 p.m.
Shoes by designers such as Christian Lacroix. Also some chic evening bags made in unusual styles by traditional embroidery methods.

70

DERBY-HANDSCHUHE   **19** N9   U 1, U 3 Stephansplatz
1, Plankengasse 5; tel. 512 57 03, and branches. Monday 12.30 p.m.–6 p.m., Tuesday to Friday 10 a.m.–6 p.m., Saturday 10 a.m.–12 noon.
Gloves and only gloves!

DIVARESE   **19** N9   U 1, U 3 Stephansplatz
1, Graben 7; tel. 512 39 99. Monday to Friday 9 a.m.–6.30 p.m., except Thursday 9 a.m.–8 p.m., Saturday 9 a.m.–12.30 p.m.
Very Italian. Attractive shoes of good quality, for teens and up.

DOMINICI   **19** N9   U 1, U 3 Stephansplatz
1, Singerstraße 2; tel. 513 45 41. Monday to Friday 9.30 a.m.–6 p.m., Saturday 9.30 a.m.–12.30 p.m.
A big range of shoes with an expensive look at a less-expensive price.

ETIENNE AIGNER   **19** O9   U 3, U 4 Landstraße/Wien Mitte
3, City Air Terminal Passage, Landstraßer Hauptstraße 2; tel. 713 12 29. Open daily including weekends and holidays, 9.30 a.m.–6 p.m.

This is the classic boutique that is seen in capital cities all over the world. It sells fairly fashionable shoes and bags.

HUMANIC   **19** N9   U 1, U 3 Stephansplatz
1, Kärntner Straße 51; tel. 512 58 92, and many branches.
Sells cheaper shoes in an enormous range of styles, but unlike its competitors it has a real sense of style.

KURT DENKSTEIN   **19** N10   U 1, U 3 Stephansplatz
1, Bauernmarkt 8; tel. 533 04 60. Monday to Friday 9.30 a.m.–6 p.m., Saturday 9.30 a.m.–1 p.m.
A major outlet for Stéphane Kelian's products. They have very good sales here if you don't mind last year's styles.

LE PETIT CHOU   **19** N9   U 1, U 3 Stephansplatz
1, Brandstätte 10; tel. 533 65 37. Monday to Friday 9.30 a.m.–6 p.m., Saturday 9.30 a.m.–1 p.m.
You can buy delightful French shoes here, at a price. Clothes are around the corner.

PALAZINA   **19** N9   U 1, U 3 Stephansplatz
1, Kärntner Straße 14; tel. 512 73 05. Monday to Friday 9 a.m.–6 p.m., Saturday 9 a.m.–12.30 p.m.
This is the young branch of the Stiefelkönig chain – very trendy.

71

REITER   **11** J11   U 6 Alser Straße
17, Schumanngasse 67; tel. 42 55 05. Monday to Friday 10 a.m.–7 p.m., Saturday 10 a.m.–1 p.m.
The hand-made shoe shop.

JEWELLERY

Vienna has so many jewellers of various descriptions that one wonders who buys it all.

CARIUS & BINDER   **19** N9   U 1, U 3 Stephansplatz
1, Kärntner Straße 17; tel. 512 67 50. Monday to Friday 9 a.m.–6 p.m., except Thursday 9 a.m.–8 p.m., Saturday 9 a.m.–1 p.m.
A well-known shop selling expensive pens, watches and jewellery.

CARTIER 19 N9 U 1, U 3 Stephansplatz
*1, Kohlmarkt 4; tel. 533 22 46. Monday to Friday 9.30 a.m.–6 p.m.,
Saturday 9.30 a.m.–12 noon.*
A large and rather splendid boutique in this wonderful street seemingly
crowned by the gold and copper-green of the Michaeler-dome.

CHOPARD 19 N9 U 1, U 3 Stephansplatz
*1, Kohlmarkt 16; tel. 533 77 58. Monday to Friday 10 a.m.–6 p.m., ex-
cept Thursday 10 a.m.–8 p.m., Saturday 10 a.m.–12.30 p.m.*
Perfumery selling costume jewellery and suchlike.

CIRO PERLEN 19 N9 U 1, U 3 Stephansplatz
1, Graben 16; tel. 533 10 64, and branches.
Very bright and sparkly jewels as well as many pearls.

DEUTSCH 19 N9 U 1, U 3 Stephansplatz
*1, Haus Hollein I, Graben 26; tel. 533 60 95. Monday to Friday 10 a.m.–
1 p.m. and 2.30–6 p.m., Saturday 10 a.m.–12.30 p.m.*
This remarkable shop was designed by the architect Hans Hollein for
the jeweller Schullin, who then sold it on (see Schullin & Söhne below).
The design is of molten metal dripping through rock and then forming
the door. Very clever though not to everyone's taste.

72

HABAN 19 N9 U 1, U 3 Stephansplatz
*1, Kärntner Straße 2; tel. 512 67 30-1210. Monday to Friday 9.15 a.m.–
6 p.m., except Thursday 9.15 a.m.–8 p.m., Saturday 9.15 a.m.–1 p.m.*
A high-street jewellery group.

KÖCHERT 19 N9 U 1, U 3 Stephansplatz
*1, Neuer Markt 15; tel. 512 58 28. Monday to Friday 9 a.m.–1 p.m. and
2–6 p.m., Saturday 9 a.m.–12 noon.*
The leading jewellers of old Vienna – in fact they were the official jewellers to the Imperial Court of Austria.

KUNZ SCHMUCKSTUDIO 19 N9 U 1, U 3 Stephansplatz
*1, Neuer Markt 13; tel. 512 71 12. Monday to Friday 9 a.m.–6 p.m.,
except Thursday 9 a.m.–8 p.m., Saturday 9 a.m.–12.30 p.m.*
A variety of jewellery with a good line in modern classics at reasonable
prices. The shiny steel and brass shopfront is also worthy of notice.

ROZET & FISCHMEISTER   **19** N9   U 1, U 3 Stephansplatz
1, Kohlmarkt 11; tel. 533 80 61. Monday to Friday 9 a.m.–1 p.m. and 2–6 p.m., Saturday 9 a.m.–12 noon.
One of Vienna's older jewellery shops distinctive for its elegance.

SCHULLIN & SÖHNE   **19** N9   U 1, U 3 Stephansplatz
1, Haus Hollein II, Kohlmarkt 7; tel. 533 90 07. Monday to Friday 10 a.m.–1 p.m. and 1.30–6 p.m., Saturday 10 a.m.–12.30 p.m.
This shop is the second designed for this jeweller by Hans Hollein (see Deutsch above). The jewellery is considered Vienna's best modern design by those in the know, and they have won the De Beer's diamond award more than once.

SWATCH SHOP   **19** N9   U 1, U 3 Stephansplatz
1, Kohlmarkt 10; tel. 533 12 00. Monday to Friday 10 a.m.–6 p.m. Saturday 9.30 a.m.–1 p.m.
An ultra modern boutique selling the ubiquitous Swatch.

WAGNER   **19** N9   U 1, U 3 Stephansplatz
1, Kärntner Straße 32; tel. 512 0 512.
All the big names in watch design: Rolex, Piaget, Baume & Mercier, among others. Also jewellery and tax-free shopping.

73

CHINA AND GLASS

There are two names that immediately spring to mind in the context of Austrian china: Gmunden and Augarten. Gmunden is attractive heavy ceramics in a variety of designs, the most common being green lines on white. It comes from the town of the same name in Upper Austrian Salzkammergut and is available at reasonable prices. Augarten, on the other hand, makes fine china, with hand-painted floral designs, also after traditional patterns. The source is in Vienna itself.

AUGARTEN   **19** N9   U 1, U 3 Stephansplatz
1, Stock-im-Eisen-Platz 3-4; tel. 512 14 94. Monday to Friday 9 a.m.–6 p.m., Saturday 9 a.m.–12.30 p.m. Or directly at 2, Wiener Porzellan-fabrik, Schloß Augarten.

KERAMIK AUS GMUNDEN **19** N9 U 1, U 3 Stephansplatz
1, Kärntner Straße 10 (Kärntner Durchgang); tel. 512 58 24. Monday to Friday 9 a.m.–6 p.m., Saturday 9.30 a.m.–12.30 p.m.
A good source of the whole range of Gmunden ceramics.

RASPER & SÖHNE **19** N9 U 1, U 3 Stephansplatz
1, Graben 15; tel. 534 33-0. Monday to Friday 9.30 a.m.–6 p.m., except Thursday 9.30 a.m.–8 p.m., Saturday 9.30 a.m.–12.30 p.m.
One of Vienna's leading names for glass, porcelain and cutlery. If it comes from Rasper & Söhne it must be the best.

ROSENTHAL **19** N9 U 1, U 3 Stephansplatz.
1, Kärntner Straße 16; tel. 512 39 94. Monday to Friday 9.15 a.m.–6 p.m., Saturday 9.15 a.m.–1 p.m.
Showrooms for the world-famous make of fine china and glass.

SLAMA **18** L8 Tram 52, 58 Neubaugasse
6, Mariahilfer Straße 71; tel. 587 36 21-0.
Probably the biggest selection of glass objects in town.

TABLETOP **18** M10 U 3 Herrengasse
1, Palais Ferstel, Freyung 2; tel. 535 42 56. Monday to Friday 9.30 a.m.–6.30 p.m., Saturday 9.30 a.m.–12.30 p.m.
An exclusive shop in a Viennese palace, selling a range of fine china

BOOKS

BATEAU LIVRE **12** M11 40A Bauernfeldplatz
9, Liechtensteinstraße 37; tel. 34 79 004. Monday to Friday 9 a.m.–6 p.m., Saturday 9 a.m.–12 noon.
By far the best place in town for French books.

BIG BEN BOOKSHOP **12** M11 Tram D Fürstengasse
9, Porzellangasse 24; tel. 319 64 12. Monday to Friday 9 a.m.–6 p.m., Saturday 9 a.m.–12 noon.
Only English books in a whole range of subjects.

BRITISH BOOKSHOP **19** N9 U 1, U 3 Stephansplatz
1, Weihburggasse 8; tel. 512 19 45; 1, Blumenstockgasse 3; tel. 513 29 33. Also at ELT centre 1, Singerstraße 30 512 26 82. Monday to Friday 9 a.m.–6 p.m., Saturday 9 a.m.–12.30 p.m.

This shop is a joint venture with the well-known Blackwell's of Oxford and offers a large range of books and magazines of all sorts. In Singerstraße they also sell books in English teaching the German language.

FREYTAG-BERNDT UND ARTARIA 19 N9 U 1, U 3 Stephansplatz
1, Kohlmarkt 9; tel. 533 20 94. Monday to Friday 9 a.m.–7 p.m., Saturday 9 a.m.–1 p.m.
Sells all manner of travel books and guides in German and some in English, but is *the* place for maps. They have an international reputation for their cartography, and even sell sea charts of all known waters.

FRICK 19 N9 U 1, U 3 Stephansplatz
1, Graben 27; tel. 533 99 14. Monday to Friday 9 a.m.–6 p.m., Saturday 9 a.m.–12.30 p.m.
Known for its books about Vienna and selection of children's and English-language books.

GALERIE WOLFRUM 19 N9 U 1, U 3 Stephansplatz
1, Augustinerstraße 10; tel. 512 53 98-0. Open Monday to Friday 9.15 a.m.–6 p.m., Saturday 9.15 a.m.–12.30 p.m.
An art bookshop with a print shop and gallery attached. It also sells postcards, prints and posters.

GEROLD 19 N9 U 1, U 3 Stephansplatz
1, Graben 31; tel. 533 50 17. Monday to Friday 8.30 a.m.–6 p.m., Saturday 9 a.m.–1 p.m.
They have an English-language department with a variety of books including literature, politics, economics and books on Vienna.

75

HEIDRICH 19 N9 U 1, U 3 Stephansplatz
1, Plankengasse 7; tel. 512 37 01. Monday to Friday 9.15 a.m.–6 p.m., Saturday 9.15 a.m.–12.30 p.m.
A good selection of secondhand and antiquarian books. They also have a good English department and a helpful staff.

HINTERMAYER 18 L8 Tram 49 Neubaugasse
7, Neubaugasse 29; tel. 930 225. Monday to Friday 9 a.m.–6 p.m., Saturday 9 a.m.–12.30 p.m.
Remaindered books at good prices, with a small selection in English. They often have good art books and picture books on Austria. Antiquarian books are a speciality.

KOSMOS, LIBRAIRIE   **19** N/O9   U 3 Stubentor

1, Wollzeile 16; tel. 512 72 21. Monday to Friday 9 a.m.–6 p.m., Saturday 9 a.m.–12 noon.

French and other foreign-language books. Also has language courses for self-tuition.

KUPPITSCH   **18** M10   U 2 Schottentor

1, Schottengasse 4; tel. 533 32 68 22/32. Monday to Friday 9 a.m.–6 p.m., Saturday 9 a.m.–12.30 p.m.

An excellent shop with very helpful staff. There is a separate English section in the same block with its entrance on Schottenbastei. Also stocks secondhand paperbacks in English.

MORAWA   **19** N/O9   U 3 Stubentor

1, Wollzeile 11; tel. 515 62-0. Monday to Friday 9 a.m.–6 p.m., Saturday 9 a.m.–1 p.m.

A good bookshop but primarily a large newsagent where back copies of recent English-language papers are available. They also run a paper/magazine delivery service.

REISEBUCHLADEN FELIX STELZER   **12** M10   U 2 Schottentor

76

9, Kolingasse 6; tel. 34 33 84. Monday to Friday 10 a.m.–6 p.m., Saturday 9.30 a.m.–12.30 p.m.

Travel books, a few in English.

SALLMAYER'SCHE   U 1, U 3 Stephansplatz
BUCHHANDLUNG   **19** N9

1, Neuer Markt 6; tel. 512 21 81. Monday to Friday 9 a.m.–6 p.m., Saturday 9 a.m.–12 noon.

Specializes in, among other things, technical literature and international film, dance and photographic magazines, many of which are in English;. Good, but comparatively expensive, secondhand section.

SHAKESPEARE & CO.   **19** N10   U 1, U 4 Schwedenplatz

1, Sterngasse 2; tel. 535 50 53. Monday to Friday 9 a.m.–7 p.m., except Thursday 9 a.m.–8 p.m., Saturday 9 a.m.–1 p.m.

English books. Pleasant shop with friendly service.

FOOD

Food shopping in Vienna is still how it should be: bread is bought at the baker's, meat at the butcher's, poultry at the poulterer's, fruit and vegetables at the market or the greengrocer's, and so on. The supermarket fulfils all your other needs but beware, their bread, meat and fruit and veg are generally of far lower quality than you would expect, as there is not the turnover to keep it all fresh.

AIDA   **19** N9   U 1, U 3 Stephansplatz
1, Stock-im-Eisen-Platz 2; tel. 512 79 25, and many branches.
A chain of cake and chocolate shops found all over Vienna, normally with a café attached.

ALTMANN & KÜHNE   **19** N9   U 1, U 3 Stephansplatz
1, Graben 30; tel. 533 09 27. Monday to Friday 9 a.m.–6.30 p.m., Saturday 9 a.m.–1 p.m.
One of the smartest places for chocolates is A&K, where they provide chocolates in unusually shaped little boxes – drums, drawers, travel chests, even a dressing table, all covered with old-fashioned paper.

ANKER
A large chain of shops selling bread and cakes on every high street and even on the smaller streets. Stocks are replenished direct from the oven three times a day.

77

BIO-GREISSLER   **11** H11   Tram 43 Wattgasse
17, Wurlitzergasse 93; tel. 462 80 65. Monday to Friday 9 a.m.–12.30 p.m. and 2.30–6 p.m., Saturday 9 a.m.–12 noon.
An excellent range of organic and wholefoods, including prepared foods. Also clothes, stationery and cosmetics.

DA CONTE   **19** N10   U 1, U 3 Stephansplatz
1, Kurrentgasse 12, entrance on Judenplatz; tel. 533 64 64. Monday to Friday 9 a.m.–7 p.m., Saturday 8 a.m.–2.30 p.m.
If you can resist filling your shopping bags with delicious treats from the mouth-watering array, you are strong willed indeed. But take care, bankruptcy looms on entering these doors. There is a catering service, takeaway food is available and delicious lunches at reasonable prices are served in the delicatessen and, in summer, in the Schanigarten. The main restaurant next door is open in the evenings.

DEMEL **19** N9 U 1, U 3 Stephansplatz
1, Kohlmarkt 14; tel. 535 55 16-0, 535 17 17-0. Daily 10 a.m.–7 p.m.
This is a Viennese institution, though today it has been somewhat taken over by tourists. It still carries the legend 'K u. K Hof-Lieferant' (supplier to the imperial and royal court), a legend designed to play on the imagination, as is its charming 20th-century baroque interior. The cakes and chocolates here are worthy of dreams, so are the prices.

DEMMERS TEEHAUS **18** M10 U 2 Schottentor
1, Mölkerbastei 5; tel. 533 59 95. Shop Monday to Friday 9 a.m.–6.30 p.m., except Thursday 9 a.m.–8 p.m., Saturday 9 a.m.–12.30 p.m.. Tee Stube Monday to Friday 10 a.m.–6.30 p.m., except Thursday 10 a.m.– 8 p.m., closed all day Saturday.
A tea shop with a strong British flavour - publicity is conducted from a red London double-decker. They sell more types of tea than you knew existed and a selection of gifts. There is a 'tea salon' upstairs.

GERSTNER **19** N9 U 1, U 3 Stephansplatz
1, Kärntner Straße 15; tel. 512 49 63. Monday to Saturday Konditorei 8.30 a.m.–7 p.m., 1st floor café 10 a.m.–7 p.m.
Home-made cakes and confectionery sold from rather prim premises.

78 **HEBEIN & SCHÜSSLER** **19** N8/O9 U 1, U 2, U 4 Karlsplatz
1, Hegelgasse 13; tel. 512 34 68. Monday to Friday 9 a.m.–6 p.m.
Coffee and tea importers – specialists in all kinds of teas. This is their retail outlet.

HEINER **19** N/O9 U 3 Stubentor
1, Wollzeile 9; tel. 512 48 38. Konditorei Monday to Saturday 8.30 a.m.– 7 p.m., Sunday and holidays 10 a.m.–7 p.m. 1st floor café Monday to Friday 11 a.m.–7 p.m., Saturday and Sunday 1.30–7 p.m.
Some say that this is the best cake shop in Vienna. It certainly is a remnant from the Empire, sporting the description 'K.u.K.' in its publicity. Upstairs has a rather better atmosphere than downstairs.

IMPERIAL TORTE SHOP **19** N8 U 1, U 2, U 4 Karlsplatz
1, Kärntner Ring 16. Kaffee Haus; tel. 501 10 313. Daily 7 a.m.–11 p.m.
This is the Imperial Hotel's outlet for its version of the much-disputed Sachertorte. See the hotel's entry (page 116) for the full story.

JULIUS MEINL AM GRABEN   19 N9   U 1, U 3 Stephansplatz
1, Graben 19; tel. 533 45 86.
Another Viennese institution; everyone who is anyone shops at Meinl am Graben. The delicatessen counter here is mouthwatering.

LEHMANN   19 N9   U 1, U 3 Stephansplatz
1, Graben 12; tel. 512 18 15. Monday to Saturday 8.30 a.m.–7 p.m.
A classic shop front – wonderfully dated – serves the usual delicious cakes etc.

NATURPRODUKTE   U 2 Schottentor
ENGELBERT PERLINGER   19 N9
1, Schottengasse 9; tel. 533 95 12.
A Perlinger shop selling wonderful breads and other prepared foods. There is a little stand-up snack bar where their delicious products can be tried, and in the back alternative beauty therapies are on offer; appointments required.
Other Perlinger branches are scattered over Vienna, the main one is at: *1, Rotenturmstraße 16-18; tel. 513 45 78*. This company is the leading mass producer of whole- and organic foods; it also sells baby food. Apart from its own attractive shops, it has outlets in most major supermarkets.

SACHER   19 N9   U 1, U 2, U 4 Karlsplatz
1, Philharmonikerstraße 4; tel. 51456. Monday to Saturday 9 a.m.–11 p.m., Sunday 3–11 p.m.
Also at 1, Kärntner Straße 38. Monday to Saturday 9 a.m.–6 p.m.
The Sacher's cake (*Sachertorte*) is more famous internationally than the other versions but is certainly no better. Cakes of various sizes packed in boxes make ideal souvenirs (also for posting home).

79

SCHÖNBICHLER   19 N9   U 1, U 3 Stephansplatz
1, Wollzeile 5; tel. 512 18 68. Monday to Friday 8.30 a.m.–6 p.m., Saturday 8.30 a.m.–12.30 p.m.
Not just more tea, but everything related to tea, including silver samovars and Chinese teapots. They are also whisky importers, and sell whisky, spirits, jams and preserves.

WILD, GEBRÜDER   19 N9   U 1, U 3 Stephansplatz
1, Neuer Markt 10–11; tel. 512 21 79. Monday to Friday 8.30 a.m.–6.30 p.m., Saturday 8 a.m.–12.30 p.m.
One of Vienna's smarter venues, offering a wide range of delicacies and wines from Austria and abroad. They also run a catering service.

ZIEGLER **19** N9   U 1, U 3 Stephansplatz
1, Kärntner Straße 44; tel. 576 81 43 and several branches. Monday to
Friday 7 a.m.–6 p.m., Saturday 8 a.m.–12 noon.
A reliable source of excellent meats, cooked and uncooked.

MARKETS

Almost every area of Vienna has its local market selling mainly fruit and
vegetables. Alongside these markets many other food shops have
sprung up providing varied and interesting produce. The First District
does not have the same small local markets, but the largest, best and
most famous market – Naschmarkt – is on its southern edge.

BRUNNENMARKT **17** K10   Tram 44 and J Brunnengasse
16, Yppenplatz/Brunnengasse.
Lovely permanent open-air market with real market stalls along
Brunnengasse, which on Saturdays is greatly enlarged by farmers from
Lower Austria putting up their stools in the adjacent Yppenplatz.

HANNOVERMARKT **13** N12   Tram 31 Brigittaplatz
20, Hannovergasse/Brigittaplatz.
Open-air market with both stalls and shops, selling nearly everything.

80 **NASCHMARKT** **18** M8   U 1, U 2, U 4 Kettenbrückengasse
7, Linke Wienzeile–Rechte Wienzeile.
Just to the south of the Opera, this is the largest and most fascinating
of all Vienna's markets. It has all sorts of shops selling both the expected
and the surprising. Vienna's best fishmongers are at the northern end
followed by the more expensive shops, but as you progress further down
the market the variety and colourfulness of the wares increase as the
price and reliability decrease.

   Many shops sell Middle-Eastern specialities: breads, olives, cheeses,
spices, etc. Temporary stalls are set up wherever there is a gap, selling wooden toys from Czechoslovakia, cheap clothes, foods and so on.
Early on Saturday mornings farmers from outside Vienna come to sell
off their produce too.

   Also on Saturdays there is a fleamarket selling secondhand clothes,
old postcards, cameras, ornaments, books, handicrafts and all manner
of junk – you may find a bargain if you are quick. Watch out for your wal-
let though, the few thieves that there are in Vienna have realized that this
is an easy place to work. Parking is usually difficult in this area.

SONNBERGMARKT **5** K13   🚌 39A Oberdöbling
19, Sonnbergplatz, Obkirchergasse.
Nice small permanent market with shops rather than stalls, selling mainly food.

GIFTS

HAAS & HAAS **19** N9   U 1, U 3 Stephansplatz
1, Stephansplatz 4; tel. 513 19 16. Shop Monday to Friday 9 a.m.–7.30 p.m., Saturday 9 a.m.–12 noon. Tea salon Monday to Friday 9 a.m.–7.30 p.m., Saturday 9 a.m.–3 p.m.
As well as offering the tired shopper a chance of a refreshing cup of tea, H & H is one of Vienna's most elegant gift shops.

KASHKA **6** L13   Tram 38 Gatterburggasse
19, Billroth Straße 52; tel. 36 92 978. Monday to Friday 10 a.m.–6 p.m., Saturday 9.30 a.m.–12 noon.
A very tasteful shop offering decorative gifts to adorn the house at reasonable prices.

KUNSTHISTORISCHES MUSEUM **18** M9   U 2 Mariahilferstraße
1, Burgring 5; tel. 523 49 03. Monday, Wednesday and Saturday 10 a.m.–6 p.m., Tuesday and Friday 10 a.m.–9 p.m.
A lovely range of specially produced gifts including scarves, china, dolls, playing cards, games, books, postcards, posters, and so on, with special items related to exhibitions on show at the time.

METZGER **19** N9   U 1, U 3 Stephansplatz.
1, Stephansplatz 7; tel. 512 34 33. Monday to Friday 9 a.m.–6 p.m., Saturday 9 a.m.–12 noon.
Looking for something typical? Here they offer those most traditional of Austrian things – Lebkuchen and candles.

NIEDERÖSTERREICHISCHES   U 3 Herrengasse
HEIMATWERK **18** M9/10
1, Hochhaus, Herrengasse 6-8; tel. 533 34 95. Monday to Friday 9.30 a.m.–6 p.m., 9.30 a.m.–1 p.m.
All sorts of Austrian souvenirs are to be found here, including traditional dress and fabrics, literature, handwork, ceramics, glass and ornaments.

OSTERMANN   **19** N9   U 3 Herrengasse
1, Am Hof 5; tel. 533 42 42. Monday to Friday 9 a.m.–6 p.m., Saturday 9 a.m.–12 noon.
Absolutely everything for the smoker in a tiny but lovely shop.

ÖSTERREICHISCHE   U 1, U 3 Stephansplatz
WERKSTÄTTEN   **19** N9
1, Kärntner Straße 6; tel. 512 24 18. Monday to Friday 9.15 a.m.–6 p.m., Saturday 9.15 a.m.–1 p.m.
More typically Austrian gifts. Excellent quality.

TAVOLA   **19** N9   U 1, U 3 Stephansplatz
1, Habsburgergasse 10; tel. 534 33-0. Monday to Friday 9.30 a.m.– 6 p.m., except Thursday 9.30 a.m.–8 p.m., Saturday 9.30 a.m.–12.30 p.m.
A fun shop full of brightly coloured kitsch bits and pieces for the kitchen and around the house. In season, a less kitsch selection of Christmas decorations. Owned by Rasper & Söhne.

TOSTMANN   U 2 Schottentor
1, Schottengasse 3a; tel. 533 53 31.
Alongside the Trachten shop, Tostmann has a charming gift shop selling all manner of folk art, including carved and painted wooden toys, music boxes and ornaments, pretty china and glass. Painted glasses are traditional in the area as are candlesticks made of Bauernsilber, which is hollow glass that has been silvered on the inside.

82

CHEMISTS

Vienna's chemists (*Apotheken*) are often in old premises, where they have been since the time that apothecaries' shops were lined with dark carved wood shelves displaying a wondrous array of bottles and porcelain pots containing all manner of lotions, salves, potions and powders. Many of them are very interesting to look around even if you don't need to buy anything. In fact, the whole interior of one of them was moved into the Technical Museum near Schönbrunn (see page 49).

ALTE LEOPOLDS APOTHEKE   **19** N9   U 1, U 3 Stephansplatz
1, Plankengasse 6; tel. 512 13 81.
Particularly charming for its shutters – when open these reveal a painted inner leaf depicting, one assumes, old Leopold himself, struggling along

a road leaning heavily on his stick. It looks as if he might be in need of his Apotheke.

APOTHEKE SCHOTTEN   **18** M10   U 1, U 3 Stephansplatz

1, Freyung 7; tel. 533 24 57. Monday to Friday 8 a.m.–12 noon and 2–6 p.m., Saturday 8 a.m.–12 noon.

Particularly notable for its exterior – it is in one of the palaces lining the Freyung.

APOTHEKE ZUM ROTEN KREBS   **19** N9   U 1, U 4 Schwedenplatz

1, Lichtensteg 4; tel. 533 67 91. Monday to Friday 8 a.m.–12 noon and 2–6 p.m., Saturday 8 a.m.–12 noon.

An excellent homoeopathic chemist where helpful advice will be given on request.

FLORISTS

MATERN NATURBLUMENSALON   **19** N9   U 1, U 3 Stephansplatz

1, Herrengasse 10; tel. 533 54 60. Monday to Friday 8 a.m.–6 p.m., Saturday 8 a.m.–1 p.m.

83

A traditional Viennese florist where they still sell the Biedermeier Strauß, a tightly bound posy of flower heads arranged in concentric circles. The shop has a delightfully fifties feel and a selection of the most elegant and beautiful plants and cut flowers.

SÄDTLER   **19** N9   U 1, U 2, U 4 Karlsplatz

1, Opernring 13; tel. 587 42 19. Monday to Friday 9 a.m.–6.30 p.m., Saturday 9 a.m.–1 p.m.

A large marble-lined showroom with beautiful flowers and plants.

TOYS

See CHILDREN.

E ating and drinking out is very popular in Vienna. It is part of Austrian culture to take the family out for lunch at the weekend, and to meet friends in *Beisln* (low-key but often highly original pubs) or at the *Heuriger* (see page 94) rather than entertaining at home. In restaurants, the emphasis is on good company, good wine, atmosphere, quantity of food and price, a dramatically different approach from many other Western European cities. In Vienna you will always eat well and at a reasonable price, though you may not get the degree of refinement found in other capitals.

An important consideration is whether there is a garden or a *Schanigarten* (tables on the pavement sheltered from the sun by sunshades and from traffic by potted plants and bushes) – on hot summer days the smoky atmosphere of *Beisln* and cafés can be almost unbearable. A *Wintergarten* is a type of conservatory, the benefits of which are obvious. More recently, many cafés and restaurants have extended into the cool, quiet courtyards of old town houses, but these gardens are required by law to close at 10 p.m. at the latest.

Austrian cuisine incorporates the best of whatever the Austro-Hungarian Empire had to offer: goulash, other paprika specialities and pancakes (*Palatschinken*) from Hungary; cakes and desserts from Bohemia (e.g. *Buchteln* and *Germknödel* – baked and boiled sweet yeast dumplings filled with jam: everybody's favourite) and pasta from Italy. No main meal would be complete if it didn't start with a good consommé garnished with Frittaten (strips of pancake), *Leberknödel* (a delicious liver dumpling) or *Fleischstrudel* (meat strudel).

American-style fast-food restaurants were slow to develop in Vienna, probably because there has been a local equivalent for a long time – the *Würstelstand*, a small kiosk selling sausages and other local specialities, such as *Leberkäsesemmel*. These kiosks are to be found on street corners all over the city and are excellent for a quick snack.

Near markets there is yet another type of outlet for snacks – the *Marktbeisln*. These are little rooms at the back of some of the more substantial stalls that provide a limited range of food, and you can even sit down to consume it.

The following are intended as a very personal selection rather than an exhaustive list of eating places in Vienna.

At the Café Central, you can take a book, discuss the world, or just enjoy the excellent Austrian dishes.

LUXURY

DA CONTE   **19** N10   U 1, U 3 Stephansplatz
1, Kurrentgasse 12; tel. 533 64 64 0. Monday to Saturday.
Luxurious restaurant specializing in Italian cuisine. Creative menu with
an excellent selection of fish dishes. Tempting, but very pricey.

DREI HUSAREN   **19** N9   U 1, U 3 Stephansplatz
*1, Weihburggasse 4; tel. 512 10 92. Daily 12 noon–3 p.m. and 6
p.m.–midnight.*
Traditional Viennese restaurant, considered one of Vienna's best. Try the
interestingly varied selection of starters. Occasionally a pianist provides
background music.

HOTEL SACHER   **19** N9   U 1, U 2, U 4 Karlsplatz
*1, Philharmonikerstraße 4; tel. 51 456. Daily 12 noon to 3 p.m. and 6 p.m.
to 11.30 p.m.*
Typically Austrian cuisine with great flair, making it competitive at an international level. Also famous for its Sachertorte – send some home as
a souvenir!

KERVANSARAY-HUMMERBAR   **19** N8   U 1, U 3 Stephansplatz
*1, Mahlerstraße 9; tel. 512 88 43. Monday to Saturday and holidays 12
noon–3 p.m. and 6 p.m.–1 a.m.*
Downstairs there is Turkish and international cuisine, upstairs an excellent
fish restaurant.

86

KORSO   **19** N8   U 1, U 2, U 4 Karlsplatz
*1, Mahlerstraße 2; tel. 51 51 60. Sunday to Friday 12 noon–2 p.m. and
7–11 p.m., Saturday 7–11 p.m.*
Behind the Hotel Bristol, this restaurants offers high-class food in an
opulent setting, accompanied by piano music.

SCHWARZENBERG   **19** N/O8   Tram D, 1, 2 Schwarzenbergplatz
*3, Schwarzenbergplatz 9; tel. 78 45 15-600. Daily 12 noon–2.30 p.m. and
6–11 p.m.*
Restaurant attached to the Hotel Schwarzenberg. Said to be the luxury
restaurant with the best view (of the palace gardens). Classic stylish interior (designed by Hermann Czech) with strong references to the
Biedermeier period.

STEIRERECK   20 P9   Tram N Rasumofskygasse
3, Rasumofskygasse 2; tel. 713 31 68. Monday to Friday 12 noon–3 p.m., 7–11 p.m.
Top restaurant serving nouvelle cuisine. Speciality *Wiener Gabelfrühstück* ('elevenses') from 10.30 a.m. *Schanigarten. Wintergarten.*

AUSTRIAN

BEI MAX   18 M9   U 3 Herrengasse
1, Landhausgasse 2; tel. 533 73 59. Monday to Friday 10 a.m.–11.30 p.m.
Good Carinthian food in two rooms: the front one decked out as a neat restaurant, the back one in simpler Austrian peasant style.

BREZELG'WÖLB   19 N10   U 1, U 3 Stephansplatz
1, Ledererhof 9 (off Judenplatz); tel. 533 88 11. Daily 11.30 a.m.–1 a.m.
Selected Austrian specialities, accompanied by classical music, in a former baker's shop with baroque decor. Candlelight and sturdy old wooden tables and benches add to the historical atmosphere.

DRESCHERL   10 H10   Tram 44 Redtenbachergasse
16, Ottakringer Straße 180; tel. 46 86 37. Monday to Wednesday 11 a.m.–midnight, Thursday to Saturday 11 a.m.–1 a.m. (closed on Saturday from May to September).
Good Viennese cuisine, with a selection of *Schnitzeln* and *Strudeln.*

87

ECKEL   5 K14   🚌 39A Daringergasse
19, Sieveringer Straße 46; tel. 32 32 18. Tuesday to Saturday 11.30 a.m.–2.30 p.m. and 6 p.m.–midnight.
Excellent creative food at reasonable prices. Very nice garden and, despite some pretentiousness, the service is excellent and friendly and the restaurant offers better value than some more luxurious places. Good selection of Austrian wines.

FIGLMÜLLER   19 N9   U 1, U 3 Stephansplatz
1, Wollzeile 5; tel. 512 61 77. Monday to Friday 8 a.m.–10.30 p.m., Saturday 8 a.m.–3 p.m.
A mixture of restaurant, *Stadtheuriger* and *Beisl*, it boasts the biggest Wiener Schnitzel in town, which is saying a lot. No beer, no coffee. Pleasant, sheltered setting with quiet *Schanigarten.*

GRIECHENBEISL   **19** N10   U 1, U 4 Schwedenplatz
1, Fleischmarkt 11; tel. 533 19 41. Daily 11 a.m.–11.30 p.m.
Despite the name, neither downmarket nor Greek, but a very solid and
slightly pricey restaurant with a lot of atmosphere in one of Vienna's oldest houses. *Schanigarten.*

LANDSKNECHT   **12** M11   Tram D Fürstengasse
*9, Porzellangasse 13; tel. 34 43 48. Monday to Friday 6.30 a.m.–2 a.m.,
Saturday and Sunday 10 a.m.–2 a.m.*
Pseudo-country interior, but good and ample Viennese and international
cuisine. *Schanigarten.*

LUSTIG ESSEN   **17** K8   U 6 Burggasse-Stadthalle
*15, Hütteldorfer Straße 4; tel. 982 51 63. Monday to Saturday 11.30 a.m.
to 11 p.m.*
How to eat your way through the whole of Viennese cuisine in one
evening! The bright idea of this restaurant is to offer lots of excellently
chosen Austrian (but also Italian) specialities in mini portions – at mini
prices (20–65 ÖS).

OFENLOCH   **19** N10   U 1, U 3 Stephansplatz
*1, Kurrentgasse 8; tel. 533 88 44. Tuesday to Thursday 10 a.m.–midnight,
Friday and Saturday 10 a.m.–1 a.m.*
Slightly (and deliberately) old-fashioned decor and atmosphere, excellent
food at moderate prices.

OSWALD & KALB   **19** O9   U 1, U 3 Stephansplatz

88 *1, Bäckerstraße 14; tel. 512 69 92. Daily 6 p.m.–2 a.m.*
Styrian wine and food, popular with media and literary people. Famous
for the invention of beef in vinegar and Styrian pumpkin-seed oil.

PETER'S BEISL   **10** H10   Tram 44 Redtenbachergasse
*16, Arnethgasse 98; tel. 46 53 75. Tuesday to Sunday 10 a.m.–2 a.m.,
except Saturday 10 a.m.–3 p.m.).*
During the daytime a fairly ordinary *Beisl*, this turns into a gourmet's delight in the evenings, thanks to the extremely high standard of both classical Viennese and nouvelle Viennese (i.e. lighter and more natural) cuisine. Very small, therefore very busy.

DER PFIFF UM DIE ECKE   **12** L11   U 6 Volksoper
*9, Wilhelm-Exner-Gasse 23; tel. 341 03 42. Monday to Friday 11 a.m.–
3 p.m. and 6 p.m.–midnight, Saturday 6 p.m.–midnight.*

Interesting nouvelle Viennese cuisine, but a very small and plain room. *Schanigarten.*

SALZAMT **19** N10   U 1, U 4 Schwedenplatz
1, Ruprechtsplatz 1; tel. 533 53 32. Daily 5 p.m.–4 a.m.
Bar at the front, restaurant at the back offering a mixture of Viennese and exotic food. Interior designed by Hermann Czech.

SCHNATTL **18** L9   U 2 Rathaus
8, Lange Gasse 40; tel. 42 34 00. Monday to Friday 11.30 a.m.–2.30 p.m. and 6 p.m.–midnight. Saturday 6 p.m.–midnight.
Very good food and pleasant service in an area that is increasingly becoming a second centre for Viennese restaurants. Excellent wine list.

SMUTNY **19** N8   U 1, U 2, U 4 Karlsplatz
1, Elisabethstraße 8; tel. 587 13 56. Daily from 9 a.m.–1 a.m.
Very pretty tiled rooms downstairs, bigger dining and function rooms upstairs. The large menu changes daily. Service is better downstairs.

STADTBEISL **19** N9   U 1, U 3 Stephansplatz
1, Naglergasse 21; tel. 533 33 23. Monday to Saturday 10 a.m.–11.30 p.m.
Old-fashioned interior with dark wood pannelling. Large range of reasonably priced Viennese dishes. *Schanigarten.*

WEINCOMPTOIRE **19** N/O9   U 1, U 3 Stephansplatz
1, Bäckerstraße 6; tel. 512 17 60. Daily 10 a.m.–midnight.
Viennese and other specialities. Over 30 different wines by the glass, and a lot more by the bottle.

89

ZUM GRÜNEN ANKER **19** N9   U 1, U 3 Stephansplatz
1, Grünangergasse 10; tel. 512 21 91. Monday to Friday 12 noon–3 p.m. and 6 p.m.–midnight.
Moderately priced Viennese restaurant with a particularly pretty *Schanigarten.*

ZUR STEIRISCHEN   Tram 71 Unteres Belvedere
BOTSCHAFT 19 O8
3, Strohgasse 11; tel. 712 33 67. Daily 11.30 a.m.–11.30 pm.
Good Styrian and international cuisine, nice garden and service. Frequented by artists and musicians. The name means 'Styrian message'.

ETHNIC

Chinese

LUCKY CHINESE **19** N9 U 1, U 3 Stephansplatz
1, Kärntner Straße 24; tel. 512 34 28. Daily 11.30 a.m.–3 p.m. and 5.30 p.m.–11 p.m.
Szechuan and Peking cuisine in what is arguably the best, and possibly the most expensive, of Vienna's 200 or so Chinese restaurants.

Greek

ACHILLEUS **19** N9 U 1, U 3 Stefansplatz
1, Köllnerhofgasse 3; tel. 512 83 28. Daily 11 a.m.–3 p.m. and 5 –11 p.m.
Tucked away in the famous 'Bermuda Triangle' area of Vienna is one of the city's best Greek restaurants, serving only Greek specialities.

KRETA **25** N7 🚌 13A Rainergasse
4, Rainergasse 12; tel. 505 32 19. Tuesday to Friday 6 p.m.–midnight, Saturday, Sunday, holidays 11.30 a.m.–3 p.m. and 6 p.m.–midnight.
Large selection of Greek dishes in a Greek atmosphere – lots of fishing nets. Usually quite crowded.

Indian

90

SHALIMAR **18** K7/L8 Tram 52, 58 Zieglergasse
6, Schmalzhofgasse 11; tel. 56 43 17. Daily 12 noon–2.30 p.m. and 6–11.30 p.m.
Excellent, if not cheap, Indian restaurant. Large garden. Surprisingly, Vienna has only about a dozen Indian and Pakistani restaurants.

Iranian

TEHERAN **6** M14 Tram 37 Barawitzkagasse
19, Hohe Warte 6; tel. 36 12 82. Daily 11.30 a.m.–11. p.m.
Very pleasant and quiet Eastern atmosphere created by a mass of Persian details in the furniture. Specialized, if not very large, menu.

Italian

DA CAPO   **19** N9   U 1, U 3 Stephansplatz
1, Jasomirgottstraße 3; tel. 535 55 44, 533 55 77. Daily 11.30 a.m.–11.30 p.m.
If you are looking for a nice pizzeria in the city centre, this is the one for you; it is directly opposite the entrance to the Stephansdom. Pleasant atmosphere and friendly service. The food is equal to the surroundings and at reasonable prices. Good wine.

LA TAVOLOZZA   **18** L10   U 2 Rathaus
8, Florianigasse 37; tel. 43 37 57. Tuesday to Sunday 6 p.m.–1 a.m.
This may be an arbitrary choice to represent the literally hundreds of good Italian restaurants in Vienna (there are about a dozen in the near vicinity of this one!), but it is worth mentioning for its Italian specialities, which do not include pizzas.

Jewish

ARCHE NOAH   **19** N9   U 1, U 3 Stephansplatz
1, Judengasse 1b; tel. 533 13 74. Sunday to Friday 11.30 a.m.–3.30 p.m. and 6.30–11 p.m., Saturday 2.30–11 p.m.
Solid Jewish restaurant with large selection of kosher dishes.

Mexican

91

MARGARITAVILLE   **18** M9   U 2 Lerchenfelderstraße
1, Bartensteingasse 3; tel. 42 47 86. Monday to Saturday 6 p.m.–2 a.m., Sunday 6 p.m.–midnight.
Large selection of Mexican food and drink in a spartanly modern room.

Spanish

BODEGA MANCHEGA   **12** M12   Tram 5, D Franz-Josefs-Bahnhof
9, Nordbergstraße 12; tel. 319 65 75. Daily 6.30 p.m.–2 a.m. (July to September 7.30 p.m.–2 a.m.).
Good Spanish (and Mexican) food in a pleasant atmosphere, despite the strange decorations. Live music from 7.45 p.m. to midnight.

ECONOMICAL

BIERHOF   19 N9   U 3 Herrengasse
1, Naglergasse 13/Haarhof; tel. 533 44 28. Monday to Saturday 4 p.m.–2 a.m. (May to September 11.30 a.m.–2 a.m.).
Lots of specialities connected with beer – beer in mixed drinks, beer in food – but also good beer-free food. Crowded, smoky atmosphere. Vegetarian dishes. *Schanigarten.*

BIEROASE   12 M11   Tram 37, 38 Canisiusgasse
9, Liechtensteinstraße 108; tel. 319 75 51. Monday to Friday 5 p.m.–midnight, Saturday 7 p.m.–midnight (in summer Monday to Friday 11 a.m.–midnight).
Viennese food, 120 sorts of beer. *Schanigarten.*

CAFÉ ZWILLINGSGWÖLB   18 M10   U 2 Schottentor
1, Universitätsstraße 5; tel. 408 53 15. Monday to Friday 9 a.m.–midnight.
A café of sorts upstairs, downstairs this is quite a reasonable restaurant with an interesting menu and, thanks to its proximity to the university, a studenty touch to it. Large selection of beers. Vegetarian dishes.

FISCHERBRÄU   U 6 Nußdorferstraße
(ERSTE WIENER GASTHOFBRÄUEREI)   12 L12
19, Billrothstraße 17; tel. 319 62 64. Daily 4 p.m.–1 a.m.
Gigantic open sandwiches and toasted sandwiches (using dark bread) but hot dishes, too. Various sorts of beer and own brewery. *Schanigarten.* Quite crowded in summer.

92

GÖSSER BIERKLINIK   19 N9/10   U 1, U 3 Stephansplatz
1, Steindlgasse 4; tel. 535 68 97. Monday to Saturday 9 a.m.–11.30 p.m.
Very good restaurant at the back, beer and snacks in the front room. Both with very nice atmosphere and excellent beer, if somewhat expensive. The ancient house alone is worth it – don't miss going to the back dining-rooms if only to admire the architecture.

PALATSCHINKENKUCHL   19 N9   U 1, U 4 Schwedenplatz
1, Köllnerhofgasse 4; tel. 512 31 05. Monday to Saturday 8 a.m.–midnight. Sunday and holidays 11 a.m.–midnight.
Unpretentious, studenty atmosphere. Serves a lot of different sweet and savoury pancakes.

SCHNITZELWIRT **18** L8 🚌 13A Westbahnstraße
7, Neubaugasse 52; tel. 93 37 71. Monday to Friday 10 a.m.–10 p.m.,
Saturday 6 p.m.–midnight (closed January to March).
Huge and very good Wiener schnitzel at reasonable prices in a crowded
and slightly shabby atmosphere.

TRZESNIEWSKI **19** N9 U 1, U 3 Stephansplatz
1, Dorotheergasse 1; tel. 512 32 91. Monday to Friday 9 a.m.–7.30 p.m.,
Saturday 9 a.m.–1 p.m.
Behind the almost unpronounceable name and the uninviting exterior
hides Vienna's most famous sandwich bar. Every sandwich 7 ÖS - standing room only.

ZUR STADT PARIS (BLAUENSTEINER) **18** L9 U 2 Rathaus
8, Josefstädter Straße 4; tel. 42 14 67. Saturday to Wednesday 9 a.m.–
12 p.m.
Very basic but reasonable restaurant. Probably one of the best examples of a traditional Viennese local eating place. Was the haunt of novelist Heimito von Doderer, of whom there is a display of memorabilia.
Schanigarten.

VIEWS AND GARDENS

HÄUSERL AM STOAN **4** G15 No public transport
19, Zierleitengasse 42a (Höhenstraße); tel. 44 13 77. Wednesday to
Sunday 11 a.m.–11 p.m.
Romantic inn (especially inside) overlooking Vienna. Big portions and
very reasonable prices. Garden suitable for even the roughest children.

SCHWEIZERHAUS **14** Q10 U 1 Praterstern
2, Straße des Ersten. Mai 116 (Prater); tel. 218 01 52. Daily 10 a.m.–11
p.m. Closed November to April.
Very popular and busy, huge beer garden with good food, draught beer,
children's playground.

ZUM JÄGERHAUS **27** T7 🚌 77A Gärtnerstraße
2, Freudenau 255; tel. 218 95 77. Wednesday to Sunday 10 a.m.–11 p.m.
Garden restaurant with a wide range of food, including lots of venison,
lamb etc. Quite reasonable prices.

HEURIGER

Main *Heuriger* districts

GRINZING Tram 38 Grinzing
Unbelievable how many taverns one can find in one place!

NEUSTIFT AM WALDE 🚌 35A to Agnesgasse
You will be spoilt for choice here.

PERCHTOLDSDORF S 1, S 2 Perchtoldsdorf
A village just outside the city, with a good number of *Heuriger*.

STAMMERSDORF Tram 31 Stammersdorf
Stammersdorf and Strebersdorf are both wine-growing villages off the beaten tourist track. They are very popular with the locals and somewhat cheaper than their counterparts in Neustift and Grinzing.

STREBERSDORF Tram 32 Edmund Havranek-Platz
Quite a number of *Heuriger*, even if you have to walk deeper into the old village from the tram terminus.

Individual *Heuriger*

The individual *Heuriger* listed here are our personal favourites.

94

10ER MARIE   16 G10 Tram J Ottakringer Straße,
Tram 10 Thaliastraße
16, Ottakringer Straße 244; tel. 46 31 16. Sunday to Thursday 3–11 p.m., Friday and Saturday 3 p.m.–midnight.
Very old, very famous and very fashionable. Probably the highest concentration of Viennese VIPs in any one place. Full restaurant.

ALTE BACKSTUBE (ANTON SPINDLER)   Tram 31 Großjedlersdorf
21, Frauenstiftgasse 4; tel. 394 34 43. Daily 4–11 p.m.
Despite the unlikely surroundings near a major road, this is a lovely quiet Heuriger, especially in summer, when you can sit in a number of open wooden pavilions in the walled garden.

ALTES PREßHAUS   5 K15 Tram 38 Grinzing
19, Cobenzlgasse 15; tel. 32 23 93. 5 p.m.–midnight. During winter closed on Sunday and Monday.

Another old and very pretty *Heuriger*. The cellar dates from 1527 so it therefore calls itself 'Oldest *Heuriger*'. One of the better ones in touristy Grinzing, again with full restaurant.

Heuriger

Soaking up the sun on the slopes of the hills north of Vienna are the vineyards of the villages of Neustift, Sievering, Grinzing and Nußdorf. The dry, white, wine produced here is served in the many *Heuriger* that line the streets of these charming villages.

The *Heuriger* is a Viennese institution, not simply a place to down a glass of wine, and it is also very popular with the Viennese and visitors alike. The term *Heuriger* originally referred to this year's wine. At the end of the 18th century, Emperor Joseph II decreed that wine growers should be allowed to sell their own wine to paying guests. The only conditions were that this should not result in a restaurant proper and the premises should not open for more than half the days of the year. The law is still in force. The *Heuriger* to whom these rules still apply have a sign saying *Buschenschank* or *ausg'steckt* and they are required to hang a sheaf of fir twigs, normally with a little lamp outside, to mark them as *Heuriger*.

Many others have long since acquired a restaurant's licence and are open most of the time. However, they retain the earthy atmosphere of the traditional *Heuriger* – bare trestle tables and benches in old farmhouses, wine served in jugs, food on a self-service counter only. Only very few, called noble-*Heuriger*, run a real restaurant kitchen, but these are normally to be avoided if you want to see the Viennese on their home ground.

The musicians in the *Heuriger* still sing the old Viennese songs, although sadly there are few purists left and a selection of international popular songs is often part of the programme. This *Schrammelmusik* – named after a famous ensemble – is generally performed by three or four men, playing fiddle, guitar and accordion, and the quality can range from the utterly dreadful to the beautifully sentimental, but it is certainly worth hearing and makes a fun night out whatever you may think of it. Anyway, a few glasses of wine will undoubtedly help to increase your enjoyment!

It may seem strange to be given directions to a village rather than to a specific *Heuriger*, but by simply going to any of the districts listed here and popping into any one of the *Heuriger* that line the streets, you are bound to find one to your liking.

BUSCHENSCHANK HUBER **4** G14 Tram 41 Pötzleinsdorf

18, Pötzleinsdorfer Straße 97; tel. 47 53 32. Tuesday to Sunday 3 p.m.–midnight (in summer daily 2 p.m.–midnight).

Very large garden and lots of rooms. Good buffet.

DIEM'AS BUSCHENSCHANK **6** M15 Tram D Beethovengang

19, Kahlenberger Straße 1; tel. 37 49 59. Monday to Friday 4 p.m.–midnight, Saturday 3.30 p.m.–midnight, Sunday 3 p.m.–midnight.

Pleasant, if nearly always crowded, *Heuriger*. Made more pleasant by having lots of little rooms which give some degree of privacy.

HEURIGER ZIMMERMANN **4** G/H14 U 6 to Nußdorferstraße
  and then 35A to Agnesgasse

19, Mitterwurzergasse 20; tel. 44 12 07. Monday to Friday 3 p.m.–midnight, Saturday, Sunday, holidays 1 p.m.–midnight.

An old farmhouse surrounded by vineyards offers shelter in the event of bad weather, but people usually come here to sit outside in the orchard and let the children play on the swings or watch the birds in the aviaries.

PASSAUERHOF **5** K15 Tram 38 Grinzing

19, Cobenzlgasse 9; tel. 32 63 45. Monday to Saturday 5 p.m.–midnight. Closed 24–28 December and 31 January to 20 February.

One of the most impressive buildings in picturesque Grinzing, this was erected in 1150 as a winery for the diocese in faraway Passau. Beautiful setting, full restaurant.

96

Stadtheuriger

A number of cellars and vaults in Vienna's city are huge *Heuriger*-type restaurants that were formerly (or still are) owned by Lower Austrian monasteries. Unlike genuine *Heuriger*, most of them run full restaurant kitchens, and serve a variety of drinks.

AUGUSTINERKELLER **19** N9 Tram 1, 2 Oper

1, Augustinerstraße 1; tel. 533 10 26. Daily 10 a.m.–midnight, Saturday 10 a.m.–1 a.m.

Atmospheric restaurant at the back; fast-food-type outlet with typically Viennese format near the entrance. Enjoy the *Heuriger*-music which starts from 6.30 p.m.

ESTERHAZYKELLER **19** N9   U 3 Herrengasse
*1, Haarhof 1; tel. 533 93 40. Downstairs Monday to Friday 11 a.m.–10
p.m.; upstairs Monday to Friday 9 a.m.–10 p.m., Saturday and Sunday
4–10 p.m.*
Cold and hot buffet, good wines, smoky atmosphere.

MELKER STIFTSKELLER **18** M10   U 2 Schottentor,
                                                U 3 Herrengasse
*1, Schottengasse 3; tel. 533 55 30. Monday to Saturday 5 p.m.–midnight,
closed Sunday and holidays.*
Huge, deep vault makes this feel like a big cave, but good food and wine.

URBANIKELLER **19** N10   U 3 Herrengasse
1, Am Hof 12; tel. 533 24 07, 533 91 02. Daily 6 p.m.–1 a.m.
Full Viennese cuisine in a beautiful baroque cellar that is fully panelled
in dark wood. Live music each evening (alternately a Hungarian violin
and accordion duo or *Schrammelmusic*, the traditional Viennese *Heuriger*
music). Not as cheap as it might be, but worth it for the music.

ZWÖLF-APOSTEL-KELLER   U 1 Stephansplatz, U 3 Stubentor
1, Sonnenfelsgasse 3; tel. 512 67 77. Daily 4.30 p.m.–midnight.
Very deep cellars with limited cuisine. More *Heuriger*-type atmosphere
and a more mixed clientele than other *Stadtheuriger* and nearly always
crowded. Try their blackcurrant wine – very good but extremely potent!

CAFÉS

In contrast to Italy, where coffee is drunk frequently throughout the day,
often without even sitting down, coffee in Austria is something to take your
time over. It comes in big cups, in many varieties, and is less strong than
espresso, although in proper cafés it is always served with a small glass
of water, and is mainly an excuse to spend hours watching the world go
by from a *Kaffeehaus* (café).

ALTE BACKSTUBE **18** L9   U 2 Rathaus
*8, Lange Gasse 34; tel. 43 11 01. Tuesday to Saturday 9 a.m.–12 p.m.,
Sunday 2 p.m.–midnight.*
Small old café at the front; bakery turned museum; incorporating a small
restaurant, at the back. This is very popular with the patrons of the nearby
Theater in der Josefstadt. After performances it instantly becomes
crowded.

ALT WIEN   **19** N/O9   U 1, U 3 Stephansplatz
1, Bäckerstraße 9; tel. 512 52 22. Monday to Friday 10 a.m.–4 a.m.,
Saturday, Sunday 3 p.m.–4 a.m.
Café bordering on *Beisl* with a deliberately decadent and dingy atmosphere. Good selection of snacks, interesting literary clientele in the
evenings, but genuine, not slick.

CAFÉ BRÄUNERHOF   **19** N9   U 1, U 3 Stephansplatz
1, Stallburggasse 2; tel. 512 38 93. Monday to Friday 7.30 a.m.–7.30
p.m., Saturday 7.30 a.m.–6 p.m., Sunday 10 a.m.–6 p.m.
Traditional Viennese café with good food, which has kept up the habit
of providing chamber music at the weekends between 3 and 6 p.m.

CAFÉ CENTRAL   **18** M10   U 3 Herrengasse
1, Herrengasse 14 (Palais Ferstel); tel. 535 41 76. Monday to Saturday
9 a.m.–8 p.m.
Re-established in the newly (1986) renovated Palais Ferstel, this has been
beautifully redecorated in an attempt to regain its former glory as the most
important of literary cafés, though it is unlikely to achieve the fame of its
predecessor, where Leon Trotsky was a regular visitor and Austrian writer
Peter Altenberg actually lived, returning to the nearby Graben Hotel only
to sleep! Good, if (by café standards) very expensive, food.

CAFÉ DOMMAYER   **22** G7   Tram 58, 60 Dommayergasse
13, Dommayergasse 1; tel. 877 54 65. Daily 7 a.m.–midnight.
Probably the most traditional Viennese coffee house outside the inner
districts. It started in 1787 as a country café and the present magnificent building dates from the early 19th century; it has served as the back-
drop for a number of romantic films of the 1930s. Slightly expensive, but
excellent café.

98

CAFÉ EILES   **18** L9   U 2 Rathaus
8, Josefstädter Straße 2; tel. 42 34 10. Monday to Friday 7 a.m.–10 p.m.,
Saturday, Sunday and holidays 8 a.m.–10 p.m.
Traditional and rather pretty bourgeois Viennese café (decor from 1933).
Famous for its political history: this is where the Nazis planned the mur-
der of Chancellor Dollfuß in 1939.

CAFÉ FRAUENHUBER   **19** N9   U 1, U 3 Stephansplatz
1, Himmelpfortgasse 6; tel. 512 43 23. Monday to Friday 8 a.m.–11 p.m.,
Saturday 8 a.m.–4 p.m.
Vienna's oldest café and probably its prettiest. Large selection of food.

CAFÉ GRIENSTEIDL   18/19 M/N9   U 1, U 3 Stephansplatz
1, Michaelerplatz 2; tel. 535 26 92. Daily 7 a.m.–midnight.
Yet another re-establishment of a formerly famous Vienna café (founded in 1847), but atmosphere is sadly lacking. Large selection of food. *Schanigarten.*

CAFÉ HAAG   18 M10   U 2 Schottentor
1, Schottengasse 2; tel. 533 18 10. Monday to Friday 9 a.m.–10 p.m., Saturday 8 a.m.–9 p.m.
Very typically Viennese café, complete with good selection of newspapers (some in English) and cakes. Large sheltered garden outside in the Schottenhof.

CAFÉ IM HAAS-HAUS   19 N9   U 1, U 3 Stephansplatz
1, Stephansplatz 12; tel. 535 39 69. Monday to Saturday 9.30 a.m.–6.30 p.m.
Only coffee and cakes, no hot food or snacks. Situated on the 6th floor of the modern and much disputed Haas-Haus; the half-circular glass wall affords a fantastic view of the Stephansdom and the square below, easily making up for what the café lacks in food and atmosphere.

CAFÉ HAWELKA   19 N9   U 1, U 3 Stephansplatz
1, Dorotheergasse 12; tel. 512 82 30. Wednesday to Saturday and Monday 8 a.m.–2 a.m., Sunday and holidays 4 p.m.–2 a.m.
Once (and possibly still) the café with the greatest concentration of artists and writers, and hence very popular with would-be artists and students. Always crowded. Its walls are hung with paintings by famous and less famous artists who couldn't pay, and some later ones seeking fame. **99**

CAFÉ KORB   19 N9   U 1, U 3 Stephansplatz
1, Brandstätte 9; tel. 533 72 15. Monday to Saturday 7 a.m.–midnight, Sunday and holidays 12 noon–9 p.m.
Café with good selection of cakes and a good, if expensive, restaurant menu. Hidden, but very central. *Schanigarten.*

CAFÉ LANDTMANN   18 M10   Tram 1, 2 Burgtheater
1, Dr-Karl-Lueger-Ring 4; tel. 533 91 28. Daily 8 a.m.–midnight.
The most prestigious (and therefore most expensive) of the Ringstraßen cafés (founded in 1873). Not only was this café favoured by Sigmund Freud but one of Arthur Schnitzler's most famous psychoanalytical stories, *Leutnant Gustl*, is set here. The Viennese come here just to be seen. Large terrace.

CAFÉ MUSEUM   **18/19** M/N8   U 1, U 2, U 4 Karlsplatz
1, Friedrichstraße 6; tel. 56 52 02. Daily 7 a.m.–11 p.m.
Traditional Viennese café, beautifully designed (by Adolf Loos in 1899) and now tastefully renovated. It used to be the favourite coffee house of Elias Canetti, winner of the Nobel Prize for Literature. Small selection of very reasonable snacks only. Traditionally literary clientele. Covered *Schanigarten*.

CAFÉ PRÜCKEL   **19** N9   U 3 Stubentor
1, Stubenring 24; tel. 512 43 39. Daily 9 a.m.–10 p.m.
Fine old Viennese café on the Ring. Renovated in 1950s style, but not too badly. Lots of newspapers. Piano music from 7 to 10 p.m. on Monday, Wednesday, Friday and Sunday. Full menu.

CAFÉ SAVOY   **18** M8   U 4 Kettenbrückengasse
6, Linke Wienzeile 36; tel. 56 73 48. Monday to Friday 6 p.m.–2 a.m., Saturday 9 a.m.–6 p.m. and 9 p.m.–2 a.m.
Beautiful building from the days of Vienna's classical historicism. No hot food. *Schanigarten.*

CAFÉ   Tram D, 1, 2 Schwarzenbergplatz
SCHWARZENBERG   **19** N8
1, Kärntnerring 17; tel. 512 73 93. Sunday to Friday 7 a.m.–midnight, Saturday 9 a.m.–midnight.
Excellent café with full menu, but somewhat hectic atmosphere. When renovated in 1979 the interior became slightly less reminiscent of a fishmonger's – but the large mirrors are still there. Terrace.

100

CAFÉ SPERL   **18** M8   57A Köstlergasse
6, Gumpendorfer Straße 11; tel. 586 41 58. Monday to Saturday 7 a.m.–11 p.m., Sunday 3–11 p.m. (Sunday closed in July and August).
Genuine old café. It was built in 1880 and hardly changed until renovation in 1983. Now it is almost too beautiful. This café was a favourite of Franz Lehár's. Very reasonable cuisine. Billiard and card tables.

CAFÉ ZARTL   **20** P9   Tram N Rasumofskygasse
3, Rasumofskygasse 7; tel. 712 55 60. Monday to Friday 8 a.m.–midnight, Saturday 8 a.m.–6 p.m. Closed in August.
Café with a lot of character. Cakes and some main courses. Snooker tables and newspapers. Former hang-out of literary and arty characters such as Robert Musil, Heimito von Doderer, Georg Eisler and Richard Tauber.

KLEINES CAFÉ   19 N9   U 1, U 3 Stephansplatz
1, Franziskanerplatz 3. Monday to Saturday 10 a.m.–2 a.m., Sunday 1 p.m.–2 a.m.
Very pretty café, designed in 1970-77 by Hermann Czech.

VOLKSGARTEN-MEIEREI   18 M9   Tram 1, 2 Bellaria
1, Im Volksgarten; tel. 533 21 05. Daily April to August 8 a.m.–9 pm., September and October 9 a.m.–9 p.m. (only in good weather).
Open-air café – quiet and with a view of some major sights.

ICE-CREAM

CALLOVI   19 N9   U 1, U 3 Stephansplatz
1, Tuchlauben 15; tel. 533 25 53. Monday to Saturday 9.30 a.m.–11.30 p.m., Sunday 10 a.m.–11.30 p.m. (April to September).
Very small but very good ice-cream parlour near the centre of the city.

GARDA-GELATERIA   U 1, U 3 Stephansplatz
HOHER MARKT   19 N10
1, Hoher Markt 4; tel. 533 32 97. Daily 9 a.m.–11 p.m.
Central ice-cream parlour with café. *Schanigarten.*

ITALIENISCHER EISSALON AM   U 1, U 4 Schwedenplatz
SCHWEDENPLATZ   19 N/O10
1, Franz Josefs-Kai 17; tel. 533 19 96. Open Monday to Friday 10 a.m.–11 p.m., Sunday 11 a.m.–11 p.m. (April to September).
Very popular ice-cream parlour, ranking high in quality.

SORBETTERIA DI RANIERI   19 N9   U 1, U 3 Stephansplatz
1, Kärntnerstraße, 28; tel. 512 31 34. Daily all year round 9 a.m.–12 midnight.
One of the few places you can find both sorbet and frozen yogurt, along with the delicious ice-creams so popular in Vienna.

TICHY   25 O5   U 1 Reumannplatz
10, Reumannplatz 13; tel. 604 44 46. Daily 10 a.m.–11 p.m. from mid-March to end of September.
Vienna's best ice-cream. Inventor of the famous *Eis-marillenknödel* (imitation apricot dumpling made from ice-cream – delicious). Always crowded, but definitely worth queuing.

Vienna might not have the swinging nightlife of other major cities, but it does have a wide variety of entertainment, some of which extends into the early hours. The main streets of the inner city pulsate with life until late, especially the 'Bermuda Triangle' area near the Rothenturmstraße.

Vienna is a relatively safe city at night, apart from the red-light districts on the Gürtel, the main road circling the city, beginning near the Westbahnhof and ending near Alserstraße, and the area around the Prater. However, it is always advisable for single women to take a cab home rather than using public transport.

Naturally enough, German is the language used in most places of entertainment. There is, however, also a good choice of cultural events in English.

THEATRE

HOW TO BOOK THEATRE TICKETS IN VIENNA

You can book tickets for the four main stages – the Opera, the Burgtheater, the Akademietheater and the Volksoper – up to one week in advance at the Bundestheaterkassen (1, Hanuschgasse 3, in the court-yard), or you can buy tickets in the afternoon (these are called *Vorverkauf*) at the theatre itself for performances during the coming week. There are several ticket agents about the town, but their prices are always considerably higher. Telephone booking is available for credit-card holders six days in advance of performance: tel. 513 1 513.

Credit cards can also be used for the Vereinigte Bühnen Wien (e.g. Theater an der Wien, Raimundtheater): tel. 599 77-19.

Tourist information on cultural events: tel. 211 14-0 or 513 88 92.

103

Theatres with English productions

INTERNATIONAL THEATRE   **12** M11   Tram D Schlickgasse
9, Porzellangasse 8; tel. 31 62 72.
This tiny theatre has an excellent reputation for both the standard of its productions and the great care with which the programme is planned.

All over Vienna you'll hear music – the Staatsoper is a particularly magnificent venue.

The season usually includes a high-brow drama, a popular whodunit or comedy and possibly an 'educational' play to bring in the schools. The annual *Christmas Carol* is rapidly becoming a Viennese tradition!

VIENNA'S ENGLISH THEATRE 18 L9 U 2 Lerchenfelderstraße 8, Josefsgasse 12; tel. 402 12 60.

Vienna's English Theatre performs a well-chosen selection of popular comedies, whodunits and serious plays. The company is based in Vienna but augments its cast with actors from English-speaking countries.

Well-known theatres – productions in German

AKADEMIETHEATER 18 L9 U 4 Stadtpark, 4A Lisztstraße 3, Lisztstraße 1; tel. 514 44-2959

The Akadamietheater is the sister theatre to the Burgtheater. The stage is somewhat smaller, and the pieces performed here tend to be more modern (though still classics in their own right) than those shown at the Burgtheater. It is the priciest of the larger Viennese theatres, but its productions are of an extremely high quality.

BURGTHEATER 18 M9 Tram 1, 2 Burgtheater 1, Dr-Karl-Lueger-Ring 2; tel. 514 44-2959.

The impressive round building opposite the Rathaus on the Ring houses Austria's National Theatre. It has been an important stage in the German-speaking world since its 18th-century beginnings and today offers modern, and sometimes provocative, drama in lively productions as well as productions of classic German and Austrian dramatists.

104

THEATER IN Tram J Lederergasse, DER JOSEFSTADT 18 L9 13A Theater in der Josefstadt 8, Josefstädter Straße 26; tel. 402 76 31-0, 402 51 27.

Possibly Vienna's most beautiful theatre and certainly one that transports you back to the turn of the century – making it a great favourite of the Viennese. The selection of plays leans heavily towards Austrian turn-of-the-century pieces (particularly Schnitzler or Hofmannsthal plays), which are extremely well performed. A night out here is definitely part of the Viennese experience – if your German is up to it!

VOLKSTHEATER 18 L/M9 U 2, U 3 Volkstheater 7, Neustiftgasse 1; tel. 523 35 01-0, 93 27 76.

Once the major stage for all important modern plays, the Volkstheater (formerly 'Deutsches Volkstheater') went through a distinct low in the 1970s and 80s. However, it is currently experiencing a boom, in terms of both quality and popularity. The range of productions is wide and includes musical classics such as Brecht's *Threepenny Opera*.

Smaller and lesser-known theatres

ETABLISSEMENT RONACHER 12 L12   U 1, U 3 Stephansplatz
1, Himmelpfortgasse 25; tel. 513 44 42.
Repeatedly closed 'for good', this once impressively decorated theatre (which played host to the Burgtheater when it was damaged during the war) is also repeatedly re-opened as a temporary standby for other stages. Most recently it helped out the Theater an der Wien with the seemingly never-ending success of *Cats*.

JURA-SOYFER-THEATER 18 L8   Tram 52, 58 Amerlingstraße
7, Neubaugasse 3; tel. 93 24 58-0.
Theatre dedicated completely to the works of Jura Soyfer (1912-1939), the Communist author killed by the Nazis in Buchenwald. His plays are naturally dominated by social criticism. In summer there is an open-air stage at 7, Spittelberggasse 7–10.

KABARET SIMPL 19 O9   U 3 Stubentor, 🚌 1A Riemergasse
1, Wollzeile 36; tel. 512 47 42.
Oldest surviving cabaret (founded in 1912), following the Viennese tradition of ironic word-play and satire rather than music and slapstick.

105

KAMMERSPIELE 19 N9/10   U 1, U 4 Schwedenplatz
1, Rotenturmstraße 20; tel. 533 28 33-0.
Belongs to the Theater in der Josefstadt and shares the same cast. Smaller scale, usually comedies.

METROPOL 11 J/K10   Tram 43 Palffygasse
17, Hernalser Hauptstraße 55; tel. 43 35 43.
Here the programme of plays, concerts, cabaret, even discussions, changes nightly. Not at all glamorous, but the quality of the entertainment is of a constantly high standard. Bar for drinks during performances.

ODEON-SERAPIONS THEATER 13 O10 Tram N, 21 Karmeliterplatz
2, Taborstraße 10; tel. 214 55 62.
The most exciting of all Viennese companies. Usually only one production
a year, but unusually adventurous and perfectionist. Predominantly mime,
therefore there is no language problem. A Serapions production could
be the highlight of your stay in Vienna!

ORIGINAL PRADLER RITTERSPIELE 19 09   U 3 Stubentor
1, Biberstraße 2; tel. 512 54 00.
Pseudo-medieval fun for all.

SCHAUSPIELHAUS 12 M11   Tram D Schlickgasse
9, Porzellangasse 19; tel. 34 01 01.
Small stage, classical chamber plays.

SCHÖNBRUNNER SCHLOßTHEATER 22 H7   U 4 Schönbrunn
13, Schloß Schönbrunn, main entrance; tel. 877 45 66.
This theatre is the only remaining baroque theatre in Vienna. It was
designed by Nicolaus Pacassi and opened in 1747. Alterations made
late that century gave the interior a more rococo style. Joseph Haydn
conducted in the theatre in 1777 and Mozart in 1786. In 1908 Franz
Joseph celebrated his 60th anniversary as emperor here with a ballet
performed by the family – 43 Habsburg archdukes and duchesses aged
from 3 to 18. Nowadays the theatre is used by the Max-Reinhardt-
Seminar as a rehearsal stage, and during the summer months members
of the Wiener Kammeroper (Viennese Chamber Opera) perform operettas and other works while the other theatres are closed (during July
and August).

106 **TSCHAUNER 16** G9/10   Tram 10 Roseggergasse
16, Maroltingergasse 43; tel. 982 46 05.
Vienna's only impromptu theatre on an open-air stage (with sliding roof,
just in case). A bar enhances the relaxed atmosphere even more. Good
fun with plenty of slapstick, but beware of Austrian dialect!

VOLKSTHEATER IN DEN AUßENBEZIRKEN
At varying venues; tel. 523 35 01.
This theatre company is part of the Volkstheater and shares its cast. It
travels into districts normally without theatrical entertainment, and at the
same time tests out new or smaller plays. Despite the venues in suburban
multifunctional halls, this company offers high-quality performances.

OPERA AND MUSIC

RAIMUNDTHEATER   23 K7   Tram 62, 65 Paulanergasse
6, Wallgasse 18–20; tel. 599 77-0.
Formerly dedicated to operettas, musicals are now performed here as
well. Beautiful 19th-century theatre makes a night out here something
special.

SCHÖNBRUNNER SCHLOßTHEATER (See Theatres.)

STAATSOPER   19 N8   Tram 1, 2 Oper
1, Opernring 2; tel. 514 44-2959.
From September to the end of June, Vienna's world-famous opera house
offers you the opportunity to hear top-quality opera performed by world-
famous opera singers accompanied by the Vienna Philharmonic
Orchestra under the baton of their resident conductor or a well-known
guest. Seats are very expensive, but it is possible to have one of the best
positions, both aurally and visually, by obtaining one of the incredibly
cheap tickets for standing room. Join the queue that forms at the side
entrance about two hours or so before the opera is due to begin.
Regulars take a scarf to mark their chosen standing place and then hurry
off to grab a bite to eat in one of the neighbouring cafés!

THEATER AN DER WIEN   18 M8   U 1, U 2, U 4 Karlsplatz
6, Linke Wienzeile 6; tel. 588 30-0, 587 82 14.
Formerly a reputable stage for plays of all sorts, the house has now
turned into a home for West End and Broadway musicals. Productions
are often performed in both German and English, so check beforehand
which is on offer tonight!

VOLKSOPER   12 L11   U 6, Tram 40, 41, 42 Volksoper
9, Währinger Straße 78; tel. 514 44-2959.
The Volksoper is the moneyspinner of the four state-owned stages because of its excellent performances of all the popular operettas and operas. This is the place to come for your favourite Strauss, Lehar or Kálmán
operetta or Mozart opera.

WIENER KAMMEROPER   19 N10/O9   U 1, U 4 Schwedenplatz
1, Fleischmarkt 24; tel. 512 01 00-31.
Serves as the stage for talented young singers, actors and dancers prior
to entering the Volksoper or the Staatsoper. The repertoire tends toward
the classical (sometimes in shortened versions), but includes spoofs of
well-known works as well as forgotten baroque operas.

CINEMA

Vienna is extremely well provided with cinemas – all current releases are on offer somewhere in the city, in English or other original language as well as dubbed into German.

Most of the big cinemas are split up into several smaller auditoriums, so make sure you are getting tickets for the right film. Tickets are usually half price on Monday nights.

Cinemas showing films in their original language (usually English)

BURG-KINO   18 M8   Tram 1, 2 Babenbergerstraße
1, Opernring 19; tel. 587 94 06.
Two screens. Films almost always in English. They include old classics (like *The Third Man*) in their programme for tourists in summer. Not the most elegant of cinemas, but the first to show films in the original language and an excellently varied programme.

CINE CENTER   19 N10   U 1, U 3 Stephansplatz
1, Fleischmarkt 6; tel. 533 24 11.
Four screens. New films, occasionally in English.

DE FRANCE   18 M10   U 2 Schottentor
1, Schottenring 5; tel. 34 52 36.
Two screens. New films, occasional reruns, normally only films in English.

FILMHAUS STÖBERGASSE   24 L/M6   🚌 14A Fendigasse
5, Stöbergasse 11-15; tel. 55 56 05.
Reruns and film seasons of avant-garde and art films, normally in the original language.

ÖSTERREICHISCHES   U 1, U 3 Stephansplatz
FILMMUSEUM   19 N9
1, Augustinerstraße 1; tel. 533 70 54-0. Open October to May.
Officially for members only, but membership is cheap and instant. Short film seasons of one to two weeks dedicated to individual directors, countries, genres, actors, even collections of documentary material. Films are usually shown in the original language with subtitles or hand-outs. It is well worth joining if you are interested in good films.

STAR-KINO **18** L9 🚌 48A Zieglergasse
7, Burggasse 71; tel. 93 46 83.
Reruns and film seasons, usually in the original language, all seats same price. Run-down exterior.

Cinemas showing films dubbed into German

ERIKA-KINO **17** K9 Tram 5 Lerchenfelder Straße
7, Kaiserstraße 44–46; tel. 93 13 83.
Vienna's oldest cinema (1900). Reruns only, especially of classics such as Monty Python, Woody Allen, etc.

KÜNSTLERHAUS-KINO **19** N8 U 1, U 2, U 4 Karlsplatz
1, Akademiestraße 13; tel. 505 43 28.
Major new films.

URANIA KINO **19** O10 Tram 1, 2 Julius Raab-Platz
1, Uraniastraße 1; tel. 712 61 91.
There are single performances or reruns of older films, normally those not shown in commercial cinemas, performed in this lecture hall/stage/cinema dedicated to popular education.

VOTIV-KINO **12** M10 U 2 Schottentor
9, Währinger Straße 12; tel. 34 35 71.
Two screens. High standard of films, old and new. On Thursday, Saturday and Sunday there are children's films at 4 p.m. Their Kinderkinoklub also organizes film days or weeks with shows, discussions and workshops.

109

CONCERT HALLS

Vienna is a city of music and there are concerts every night from mid-September to the end of June somewhere in the city. An all-inclusive list is virtually impossible, so here are the main halls for classical music. Concerts at smaller venues are given in the monthly programme available from the Tourist Information Office either at the Rathaus (Town Hall) or else in the Opernpassage, the subway near the opera house leading to the Karlsplatz. The main orchestras and choruses have their summer break during July and August, but there are still lots of events, featuring either visiting orchestras and choirs or else the younger generation of the established houses.

GROSSER SENDESAAL DES ORF 19 N7   U 1, U 2, U 4 Karlsplatz
4, Argentinierstraße 30a; tel. 501 01-0.
A modern concert hall in the same building as the Austrian radio station ORF. It is the home of the ORF Symphony Orchestra.

HOBOCKENSAAL 19 N9   U 1, U 3 Stephansplatz
1, Augustinerstraße 1; tel. 534 10-307.
A medium-size concert hall that has connections with the musical collection of the Austrian National Library.

KONZERTHAUS 19 O8   U 4 Stadtpark
3, Lothringerstraße 20; tel. 712 12 11.
Three concert halls are united in this building. The Großer Saal (Grand Hall) serves for all major orchestral performances; the Mozartsaal is a galleried concert hall for chamber orchestras; the small Schubertsaal stages chamber music, modern music and Lieder evenings. During the summer months there are twice-weekly concerts of Mozart selections performed in period costume. These are aimed at tourists who might not have the chance to hear full concerts.

MUSIKVEREIN 19 N8   U 1, U 2, U 4 Karlsplatz
1, Bösendorferstraße 12; tel. 505 81 90.
Two concert halls are contained in the home of the Vienna Philharmonic Orchestra. The larger is the Großer Saal (Grand Hall), which is the beautiful setting of the world-famous Vienna New Year Concert and is also the venue of the annual Philharmonic ball. The smaller Brahmssaal is a galleried hall used for chamber music and ancient music; musicians say that the Brahmssaal has the best acoustics of all Vienna's concert halls.

110

ÖSTERREICHISCHE   Tram 1, 2 Oper
GESELLSCHAFT FÜR MUSIK 19 N9
1, Hanuschgasse 3; tel. 512 42 99.
Very small concert room for chamber music or song evenings.

PALAIS PALFFY 19 N9   U 1 Stephansplatz
1, Josefsplatz 6; tel. 512 56 81.
Small concert hall, also used for various other functions.

JAZZ AND OTHER LIVE MUSIC

ARENA   26 R7   🚌 80A Franzosengraben
3, Baumgasse 80; tel. 78 85 95.
Controversial multipurpose music and arts centre.

JAZZLAND   19 N/O10   U 1, U 4 Schwedenplatz
1, Franz-Josefs-Kai 29; tel. 533 25 75.
The most established of all Viennese jazz venues. It attracts the better-known bands and leans towards traditional rather than modern jazz. Nice atmosphere in a cellar under Ruprechtskirche.

JAZZSPELUNKE   18 L/M8   U 4 Kettenbrückengasse
6, Dürergasse 3; tel. 57 01 26.
Relatively new jazz venue, featuring all sorts of jazz.

OPUS ONE JAZZ CLUB   19 N8   U 1, U 3 Stephansplatz
1, Mahlerstraße 11; tel. 513 20 75.
Jazz club and venue for other types of modern music concerts.

PAPAS TAPAS   19 N/O8   Tram D, 1, 2 Schwarzenbergplatz
4, Schwarzenbergplatz 10; tel. 65 03 11.
In the same house as the Atrium disco, this place offers Spanish snacks together with Austrian and other jazz.

RINCON ANDINO   18 L7   U 4 Kettenbrückengasse
6, Münzwardeingasse 2; tel. 56 71 28.
Bar and venue for concerts, performances and cabarets, for which you have to pay separately from the entrance fee. In summer there are sometimes performances of children's theatre.

111

SZENE WIEN   26 Q5   Tram 71 Kopalgasse
11, Hauffgasse 26; tel. 74 33 41.
Venue for pop concerts.

TUNNEL   18 L10   U 2 Rathaus
8, Florianigasse 39; tel. 42 34 65.
Live jazz and folk music in the cellar, at very cheap prices.

WUK (VEREIN ZUR SCHAFFUNG OFFENER   Tram 37, 38, 40, 41,
KULTUR- UND WERKSTÄTTENHÄUSER) 12 L11   42 Spitalgasse
9, Währingerstraße 59.
Multipurpose youth centre with facilities for rock concerts.

DISCOS AND NIGHTCLUBS

As in other cities, discos in Vienna tend to open late and liven up even later. But there are enough to satisfy most requirements, and some have a particularly Viennese touch to them, such as the Café Volksgarten.

ATRIUM   **19** N/O8   Tram D, 1, 2 Schwarzenbergplatz
4, Schwarzenbergplatz 10; tel. 505 35 94. Sunday to Thursday 8.30 p.m.–2 a.m., Friday and Saturday 8 p.m.–4 a.m.
A disco for those under 25; popular with students.

CAFÉ VOLKSGARTEN   **18** M9   Tram 1, 2 Bellaria
1, Burgring 1; tel. 533 05 18. Sunday to Thursday 8 p.m.–2 a.m., Friday, Saturday 8 p.m.–4 a.m.
An open-air dance floor in a very romantic setting under old trees is a delightful feature here, though there is a pleasant indoor dance floor as well. 'Soul Seduction' evening on Monday is particularly popular.

CHATTANOOGA DANCING   **19** N9   U 1, U 3 Stephansplatz
1, Graben 29a; tel. 533 50 00. Daily 8.30 p.m.–4 a.m.
Disco with live music.

DISKOTHEK U 4   **26** H/J6   U 4 Hietzing
112 *12, Schönbrunnerstraße 222; tel. 85 83 07. Daily 11 p.m.–4 a.m.*
Disco for the indefatigable. Clientele from punk onward.

EDEN-BAR   **19** N9   U 1, U 3 Stephansplatz
1, Liliengasse 2; tel. 512 98 45. Daily 11 p.m.–3 a.m.
Live dance music with a respectable noise level. If the photographer thinks you merit it, you might get your photograph taken and added to the selection in the display cases outside.

P1   **19** N9/10   U 1, U 4 Schwedenplatz.
1, Rotgasse 9; tel. 535 99 95. Daily 9 p.m.–4 a.m.
A big dance floor with a lively atmosphere and many students.

SPLENDID   **19** N9   U 1, U 3 Stephansplatz
1, Jasomirgottgasse 3; tel. 535 26 21. Thursday to Saturday 10 p.m.–4 a.m.
Definitely the trendy place to be seen, with many well-known personalities as regulars. Dancing to the latest pop and disco hits.

WALZERSCHIFF DDS   U 1, U 4 Schwedenplatz
'JOHANN STRAUß'   **19** O10
1, Schwedenplatz/Donaukanal; tel. 533 93 67. Open daily, music from Tuesday to Sunday 8.30–9.30 p.m. and 10–11 p.m.
Waltzing on an old Danube steamer to a live four-piece band; very nice for those whose mobility (or hearing) is past discos. Very reasonable package prices including dinner.

BARS

AMERICAN KÄRNTNERBAR   U 1, U 3 Stephansplatz
(LOOS BAR)   **19** N9
1, Kärntner Straße 10, Kärntner Durchgang; tel. 512 32 83. Sunday to Thursday 6 p.m.–2 a.m., Friday to Saturday 7 p.m.–4 a.m.
Designed in 1908 by Adolf Loos, this is a famous example of the use of minimal space with visual enlargement, using mirrors, marble and mahogany. It is advisable to book a table even though it only serves drinks.

KIX BAR   **19** N9   U 1, U 3 Stephansplatz
1, Bäckerstraße 4; tel. 513 79 35. Daily 8 p.m.–2 a.m.
Walking into this bar is like stepping into an abstract painting. The entire bar is painted in a colourful geometric design, but if you don't like orange, you're in trouble.

113

ROTER ENGEL   **19** N10   U 1, U 4 Schwedenplatz
1, Rabensteig 5; tel. 535 41 05. Sunday to Thursday 3 p.m.–3 a.m., Friday and Saturday 3 p.m.–4 a.m.
Good live pop music with lively atmosphere and interesting modern design, especially on the façade outside.

WUNDERBAR   **19** O9   U 1, U 4 Schwedenplatz
1, Schönlaterngasse 8; tel. 512 79 89. Daily 4 p.m.–2 a.m.
Designer-styled bar created in revitalized house, ironically commenting on Viennese neo-Gothic architecture with false vaulting and wooden ribs.

Despite being a major tourist centre, Vienna does not have the seemingly unlimited supply of hotel rooms found in many European cities; standards are, however, comparable. The shortage of accommodation, particularly during peak season – Christmas and New Year, and from Easter to the end of September – does mean that booking is advisable. Bookings may be made by telephone, fax or letter, and are binding for hoteliers and their clients alike, even if not confirmed in writing.

The hotels are grouped in price ranges, and rates given are per room per night. En-suite facilities are included in the price where applicable. Taxes and extra charges are also included in the given price, unless stated, but please check. Please note that many hotels impose a high surcharge on the price of telephone calls.

Breakfast is usually included and is generally a buffet of various cold meats and cheeses, cereals, bread, rolls and jam and coffee.

We have followed the star classification system used by the Vienna Tourist Board. The categories of hotel – *Hotel*, *Pension*, *Saison-Hotel* – each have different requirements determining the number of stars they achieve, which means that one category is not comparable with another even when both have the same number of stars.

Hotels, as in other countries, tend to be larger establishments and offer more facilities than merely bed and breakfast. These may be restaurants, bars, lobbies, lounges, saunas and fitness facilities.

Pensions (guest houses) are smaller and often family-run establishments offering fewer extras. These are often in blocks of flats or offices, and do not have restaurants or other social facilities.

Saison-Hotels (season's hotels) are only available in summer as they tend to be student hostels during term-time. The standard is basic and rooms tend to be somewhat spartanly furnished, though many do include an en-suite bathroom.

One area that you should be wary of is the Gürtel (ring road): not only does traffic whizz past at all hours of the day and night, but also it is the red-light district. Nevertheless, even in this area, Vienna is not a dangerous place to stay.

The whole city has excellent public transport, including a night bus service, so you can always get back to your hotel even if you do not want

The Sacher Hotel fulfils all that its reputation promises.

to take a taxi. Parking in the centre of Vienna is a problem, as only short-term parking is usually allowed. If your hotel is in the centre, the receptionist will tell you where parking is available.

Other hotels may be found in the Vienna Tourist Board's guide Hotels & Pensionen, which is freely available at tourist and travel agencies.

TOP PRICE (OVER 3,000 ÖS)

AMBASSADOR ***** **19** N9 U 1, U 3 Stephansplatz
1, Kärntnerstraße 22/Neuer Markt 5; tel. 514 66; telex 111906; fax 513 29 99. 107 rooms. Double 3,150–3,900 ÖS. Single 2,400 ÖS. Breakfast included.
A traditional Viennese-style hotel in an excellent position.

BRISTOL ***** **19** N8 U 1, U 2, U 3 Karlsplatz
1, Kärntnerring 1; tel. 515 16; telex 112474; fax 515 16-550; cable Bristotel Wien. 146 rooms. Double 3,600 –5,000 ÖS. Single 2,700 –3,900 ÖS. Breakfast included.
One of the elegant hotels on the Ringstraße.

IM PALAIS U 1, U 2, U 3 Karlsplatz
SCHWARZENBERG ***** **19** N/O8
3, Hotel im Palais Schwarzenberg, Schwarzenbergplatz 9; tel. 78 45 15; telex 136124; fax 78 47 14. 38 rooms. Double 3,000–5,300 ÖS. Single price on request. Breakfast not included.
Arguably Vienna's most elegant and sought-after hotel and restaurant are in one wing of the Schwarzenberg Palace (see page 25). The rooms are decorated and furnished in keeping with the character of the palace and the hotel contains works by Rubens and by several lesser-known artists.

116 **IMPERIAL** ***** **19** N8 Tram 1, 2 Oper
1, Kärntnerring 16; tel. 501 10; telex 112630; fax 501 10-410; cable Imperialhotel. 145 rooms. Double 3,900–6,500 ÖS. Single 3,100–3,600 ÖS.
The Imperial was opened in 1873 by Emperor Franz Joseph and was the hotel to the imperial court. It is known for its cake, the Imperial Torte, and disputes the Hotel Sacher's claim to the original recipe for this delicious chocolate cake, though the Sacher calls its identical cake the 'Sachertorte'. Do not be surprised if you find an armed police guard outside when you arrive – it simply means that some visiting dignitary is sharing the hotel with you.

INTER-CONTINENTAL WIEN ***** **19** O8   U 4 Stadtpark
3, Johannesgasse 28; tel. 711 22-0; telex 131235; fax 713 44 89. 498 rooms. Double 2,750–3,850 ÖS. Single 2,300–3,350 ÖS. Breakfast included.
Airline check-in from the hotel for Austrian Airlines, SAS, Finnair and Swissair.

MARRIOTT HOTEL ***** **19** O9   U 3 Stubentor
1, Parkring 12a; tel. 515 18-0; telex 112249; fax 515 18-6736. 304 rooms. Double 2,700–3,900 ÖS. Single 2,500–3,300 ÖS. Breakfast not included.
Another in this enormous chain catering for the business traveller. The hotel was built quite recently in a distinctive post-modernist style; it is on the Ringstraße opposite the Stadtpark.

PLAZA WIEN ***** **12** M10   U 2 Schottentor
1, Schottenring 11; tel. 313 90-0; telex 135859; fax 313 90-160; cable Plazahil. 252 rooms. Double 3,900–4,400 ÖS. Single 3,400–3,900 ÖS. Breakfast not included.
The Plaza is part of the Hilton group but has more character than that would usually denote. Decorations are partly ultramodern, partly Vienna 1900 – the latter in keeping with the fact that there has been a hotel on this site since 1873.

SACHER ***** **19** N9   Tram 1, 2 Oper
1, Philharmonikerstraße 4; tel. 514 56; telex 12520; fax 514 57-810; cable Sacherhotel. 123 rooms. Double 3,200–4,600 ÖS. Single 1,600–2,100 ÖS. Breakfast included.
This, probably Vienna's best-known hotel, is famous for its chocolate cake, over which there is a long-standing dispute. The Sacher claims to have produced the original and, of course, the best, as does the Imperial. It is a hotel with much character and style, situated next to the Vienna Opera.

117

SAS PALAIS HOTEL ***** **19** O9   U 3 Stubentor
1, Im Palais Henckel von Donnersmarck, Weihburggasse 32/Parkring; tel. 515 17-0; telex 136127; fax 512 22 16. 310 rooms. Double 3,800 ÖS. Single 2,950 ÖS. Breakfast not included.
This hotel, located in one of the palaces of the Ringstraße opposite the Stadtpark, has more of the atmosphere of imperial Austria than do some of Vienna's other top hotels. It also offers airline check-in for AUA, Finnair, SAS, Swissair.

EXPENSIVE (2,000–3,000 ÖS)

BIEDERMEIER IM SÜNNHOF ****   **19** O/P9   U 3, U 4 Wien Mitte
3, Landstraßer Hauptstraße 28/Ungargasse 13; tel. 716 71-0; telex 111039; fax 75 55 75-503. 204 rooms. Double 2,150 ÖS. Single 1,850 ÖS. Breakfast included.
A typically Viennese, or Biedermeier, hotel in a pretty old town house. The Sünnhof benefits from a convenient position near the city air terminal, and an attractive shopping arcade.

DE FRANCE *****   **18** M10   U 2 Schottentor
1, Schottenring 3; tel. 34 35 40, 34 56 01; telex 114360; fax 31 59 69; cable Francehotel. 220 Rooms. Double 2,400–2,900 ÖS. Single 1,685–2,035 ÖS. Breakfast included.
Another of Vienna's smart Ringstraße hotels, in a convenient location for both business executive and tourist. The decor is cleverly styled to include aspects of the famous Viennese artistic movements from earlier this century. The hotel is not known for its efficiency in the laundry department.
    The Hotel de France is next to the Kino de France, where English and French films are shown.

GARTEN HOTEL   S 45, 🚌 35A Krottenbachstraße
GLANZING ****   **4/5** H13
19, Glanzinggasse 23; tel. 470 42 72; fax 470 42 72-14. 20 rooms. Double 1,880 ÖS. Single 1,180 ÖS. Breakfast included.
A pleasant hotel in one of Vienna's smartest outlying residential districts where many a family has lodged very happily. It is particularly welcoming to children and has a garden in which they are free to play. Great breakfasts.

KÖNIG VON UNGARN ****   **19** N/09   U 1, U 3 Stephansplatz
1, Schulerstraße 10; tel. 515 84-0; telex 116240; fax 515 84-8. Double 1,950–2,300 ÖS. Single 1,500–1,900 ÖS. Breakfast included.
An excellent position, a pretty 17th-century Viennese house in a small, quiet street, and a good restaurant distinguish this small hotel.

118

PARKHOTEL SCHÖNBRUNN ***** **22** G7 U 4, Tram 10, 58 Hietzing
13, Hietzinger Hauptstraße 10–20; tel. 878 04; telex 132513/132151; fax 828 42 82; cable Parkhotel. 500 rooms. Double 1,990–3,200 ÖS. Single 1,315–1,925 ÖS.
Built as the Emperor Franz Joseph's guesthouse, Vienna's largest ho-

tel lies alongside the Palais Schönbrunn. Renovated in the 1950s, it is typical of fifties Vienna with much atmosphere and charm. Today, it is considered by the Viennese as a pleasant, old-fashioned place to eat. Its location is not central.

RAMADA ***** **23** J6   U 4 Meidlinger Hauptstraße
1, Linke Wienzeile/ Ullmannstraße 71; tel. 85 04-0; telex 112206; fax 85 04-100. 310 rooms. Double 1,850–2,450 ÖS. Single 1,550–2,150 ÖS.
A modern hotel not far from Schönbrunn and with easy access to public transport.

VIENNA HILTON ***** **19** O9   U 3, U 4 Wien Mitte
3, Am Stadtpark; tel. 717 00-0; telex 112474; fax 713 06 91. 603 rooms. Double 2,620 ÖS. Single 2,190–2,850 ÖS. Breakfast not included.
The Hilton is part of the same complex as the City Air Terminal and a shopping mall. It is also just by the Stadt Park.

MEDIUM PRICE (1,500–2,000 ÖS)

ALBA ACCADIA **** **24** M7   U 4 Pilgramgasse
5, Margaretenstraße 53; tel. 588 50; telex 113264; fax 588 50-899. Double 1,990 ÖS. Single 1,550 ÖS. Breakfast included.
Part of a small, modern hotel chain.

ALBA HOTEL PALACE **** **24** M7   U 4 Pilgramgasse
5, Margaretenstraße 92; tel. 55 46 86; telex 114321; fax 55 46 86-86. Double 1,990 ÖS. Single 1,550 ÖS. Breakfast included.
Part of the same small, modern hotel chain as the Alba Accadia.

ALPHA *** **12** M11   Tram 37, 38, 40, 41, 42 Boltzmanngasse
9, Boltzmanngasse 8; tel. 319 16 46; telex 115749; fax 31 42 16; cable Alphahotel. 70 rooms. Double 1,500 ÖS. Single 1,105 ÖS. Breakfast included.
Pleasant, modern hotel near the US embassy and the Modern Art Museum. No restaurant.

119

AM STEPHANSPLATZ **** **19** N9   U 1, U 3 Stephansplatz
1, Stephansplatz 9; tel. 534 05-0; telex 114334; fax 534 05-711. 62 rooms. Double 1,660–2,060 ÖS. Single 1,120–1,350 ÖS. Breakfast included.
An unprepossessing building in an excellent position facing the Stephansdom.

ANANAS ****   24 L7   U 4 Pilgramgasse

5, Rechte Wienzeile 93–95; tel. 55 56 21; telex 131970; fax 54 42 42. 525 rooms. Double 1,740 ÖS. Single 1,100 ÖS. Breakfast in room included.
Outside distinctively Viennese *Jugendstil*, inside a pleasant modern hotel. It is in a convenient position for the U-Bahn to both the First District and Schönbrunn, and about a 10-minute walk away from the Mariahilfer Straße shopping area.

CLIMA VILLENHOTEL *****   6 M15   S 40, Tram D Nußdorf

19, Nußberggasse 2c; tel. 37 15 16, 37 13 49; telex 115670; fax 37 13 92. 60 rooms. Double 1,785–2,075 ÖS. Single 1,365–1,625 ÖS. Breakfast included.
This hotel has a unique location among the vineyards of the Wienerwald (Vienna Woods) in a lovely district where Beethoven lived for several years. It is certainly not near the centre, but provided this is not too important, the charms of its location and the unusually polite and helpful service are ample compensation, not to mention the fact that it is the only 5-star hotel in this price category. Parking is freely available.

COTTAGE HOTEL ****   12 K12   Bus 40A Cottagegasse

19, Hasenauerstraße 12; tel. 319 25 71; telex 134146; fax 31 25 71-10. 23 rooms. Double 1,750 ÖS. Single 1,150 ÖS. Breakfast included.
The Cottage area is interesting because its 'cottages' are far from what are commonly known as such – the 19th-century Viennese developer had a rather grander town house in mind than the humble British cottage. The hotel comes with a strong recommendation, though it does not have a restaurant and is not near the centre. Parking is freely available. Apartments are also available for families or for a longer stay.

EUROPA ****   19 N9   U 1, U 3 Stephansplatz

1, Kärntnerstraße 18/ Neuer Markt 3; tel. 515 94-4; telex 112292. 100 rooms. Double 1,300–2,500 ÖS. Single 970–1,500 ÖS. Breakfast included.
Clean, modern and in an excellent position for most pursuits in Vienna.

HOTEL REGINA ****   12 M10   U 2 Schottentor

9, Rooseveltplatz 15; tel. 42 76 81-0; telex 114700; fax 48 83 92. 250 rooms. Double 1,900 ÖS. Single 1,320 ÖS.
Hotel dating from the turn of the century, right next to Votivkirche, with a large restaurant serving seasonal specialities.

K & K PALAIS ****   **19** N10   U 2, U 4 Schottenring
1, Rudolfsplatz 11; tel. 533 13 53; telex 134049; fax 533 13 53-70. 66 rooms. Double 1,420–1,820 ÖS. Single 1,050–1,390 ÖS. Breakfast included.
A little cheaper than other 4-star hotels because of its position at the quieter end of the First District. The building itself was the home of Katharina Schratt, actress and intimate friend of Emperor Franz Joseph.

KAISER FRANZ JOSEF ****   **5** K14   S 45 Oberdöbling
19, Sieveringer Straße 4; tel. 32 73 500; telex 116982; fax 32 73 55. Double 1,920 ÖS. Single 1,420 ÖS. Breakfast included.
This is both a pleasant, modern hotel in a residential area and an 'Appartement-Residenz', where a small, fully equipped apartment can be taken on for a minimum of 4 weeks.

KAISERIN ELISABETH ****   **19** N9   U 1, U 3 Stephansplatz
1, Weihburggasse 3; tel. 515 26; telex 112422; fax 515 26-7; cable Elisabethotel. 62 rooms. Double 1,500–1,900 ÖS. Single 1,150–1,250 ÖS. Breakfast included.
This hotel is an early-19th-century building with a typical Biedermeier interior at the very heart of the First District. It offers its clients style and comfort at a very reasonable price.

KAISERPARK SCHÖNBRUNN ****   **23** H6   U 4 Schönbrunn
12, Grünbergstraße 11; tel. 83 86 10; telex 134754; fax 83 81 83. 45 rooms. Double 1,400–1,800 ÖS. Single 1,050–1,250 ÖS. Breakfast included.
An old-fashioned Viennese hotel, with plenty of dark wood, plush seating, patterned wallpapers and Turkish rugs on the floor.

NOVOTEL WIEN AIRPORT ***   S 7 Flughafen Schwechat
Flughafen Schwechat; tel. 77 66 66; telex 111566; fax 77 32 39. Double 1,500 ÖS. Single 1,180 ÖS. Breakfast not included.
This could not be nearer the airport terminal – you need to walk just 50 yards.

121

TREND HOTEL-DONAUZENTRUM ***/*   **9** S13   U 1 Kagran
22, Wagramer Straße 83–85; tel. 23 55 45-0; telex 113785; fax 23 55 45-183. 140 rooms. Double 1,550 ÖS. Single 1,150 ÖS. Breakfast included.
This is the nearest mid-range hotel to the United Nations building. It is part of a complex that includes one of Vienna's few shopping malls: the Donauzentrum.

ECONOMICAL (UNDER 1,500 ÖS)

ALEXANDER ***   12 M12 Tram D, 5 Franz-Josefs-Bahnhof
9, Augasse 15; tel. 34 15 08; telex 13514; fax 34 15 08-82. 54 rooms. Double 1,160 ÖS. Single 870 ÖS. Breakfast included.
Convenient for trains to the north (e.g. Prague and Berlin) and public transport in general. Part of the Austropa chain.

AM BRILLANTEN Tram 49,
GRUND ***   18 K8 🚌 38 Neubaugasse/Westbahnstraße
7, Bandgasse 4; tel. 93 22 19, 93 36 62; telex 136484; fax 96 13 30. 36 rooms. Double 1,150–1,760 ÖS. Single 760–1,300 ÖS. Breakfast not included.
Pleasantly decorated in reproduction Biedermeier.

FÜRST METTERNICH ***   24 L7/8 U 4 Pilgramgasse
6, Esterhazygasse 33; tel. 588 70; telex 113215; fax 587 52 68. 57 rooms. Double 1,100–1,540 ÖS. Single 700–990 ÖS. Breakfast included.

IBIS ***   23 K7 U 6 Westbahnhof
6, Mariahilfer Gürtel 22–24; tel. 56 56 26; telex 133833; fax 56 43 68. 341 rooms. Double 1,390 ÖS. Single 990 ÖS.
Clean, comfortable French hotel chain.

JÄGER ****   10 H10 S 45, Tram 43 Hernals
17, Hernalser Hauptstraße 187; tel. 46 41 31-0. 46 66 20-0; fax 43 89 01 150. 18 rooms. Double 1,300 ÖS. Single 900 ÖS. Breakfast included.
A 4-star hotel at such a low price is indeed unusual. It is in a good shopping street, in a pleasant area, but not central.

KAHLENBERG *** 🚌 38A Kahlenberg
19, Josefsdorf 1; tel. 32 12 51-75; telex 111632; fax 32 12 51-33. 31 rooms.
No prices are available as the hotel is about to be renovated and it is uncertain when exactly it will be reopened. It is, however, in a truly astonishing position, looking out from the top of a hill in the Wienerwald with the whole of Vienna to the east laid out like a map at your feet.

122

KÄRNTNERHOF ***   19 N/O9 U 1, U 3 Stephansplatz
1, Grashofgasse 4 (off Köllnerhofgasse); tel. 512 19 23; telex 112535; fax 512 19 23. 43 rooms. Double 1,260 ÖS. Single 960 ÖS. Breakfast included.

An attractive old building in a lively part of the First District, though the hotel itself is in a quiet cul-de-sac next to the Heiligenkreuzerhof. An excellent location.

PAPAGENO ***   19 N8   U 1, U 2, U 4 Karlsplatz
4, Wiedner Hauptstraße 23–25; tel. 504 67 44; telex 61-3222204; fax 65 67 44-22. 39 rooms. Double 1,440 ÖS. Single 480 –1,020 ÖS. Breakfast included.
A good position near the Karlsplatz and also one of Mozart's many homes.

ROSEN-HOTEL EUROPAHAUS *   U 4 Hütteldorf
14, Linzer Straße 429; tel. 97 25 38; telex 114293; fax 597 06 89-89. 22 rooms. Double 600 ÖS. Single 365 ÖS. Breakfast included.
In the park of the baroque Schloß Miller-Aichholz, now a conference centre. A good distance from the middle of Vienna.
   (Telex and fax numbers are for the hotel group's head office and are not in the hotel itself.)

SAVOY ***   18 L8   Tram 52, 58 Stiftgasse
7, Lindengasse 12; tel. 93 46 46; telex 0132491; fax 93 46 40. 43 rooms. Double 1,590 ÖS. Single 1,050 ÖS. Breakfast included.
A comfortable hotel furnished with cottagey reproduction antique furniture.

SCHLOSS   🚌 46B, 146B Schloß Wilhelminenberg
WILHELMINENBERG ***   10 F11
16, Savoyenstraße 2; tel. 45 85 03; telex 132008; fax 45 48 76. 94 rooms. Double 1,000–1,250 ÖS. Single 675–860 ÖS. Breakfast included.
This magnificent building overlooking all of Vienna also has short-term apartment accommodation and a youth hostel next door. Though in the economical category, the hotel is an impressive Schloß built in 1918 in the neo-empire style. It was once the home of the Vienna Boy's Choir. Not central.

123

WANDL ***   19 N9   U 1, U 3 Stephansplatz. 🚌 1A, 2A, 3A
1, Petersplatz 9; tel. 534 55; fax 534 55-7. 138 rooms. Double 800–1,450 ÖS. Single 450–900 ÖS. Breakfast included.
Also in Petersplatz is the beautiful Peterskirche, standing to one side of the Graben in the heart of the First District. The area is a pedestrian precinct with splendid buildings, sculptures and Vienna's smartest shops.

It is also the venue for some of the best of Vienna's many buskers and street performers. What more can you want of a location?

ZU DEN DREI KRONEN ** **18** M8 U 4 Kettenbrückengasse
4, Schleifmühlgasse 25; tel. 587 32 89; telex 112555; fax 26 90 23/75. 39 rooms. Double 1,350 ÖS. Single 940 ÖS. Breakfast included.
By the Naschmarkt, Vienna's best and largest market (see page 80).

ZUR WIENER STAATSOPER *** **19** N9 U 1, U 2, U 4 Karlsplatz
1, Krugerstraße 11; tel. 513 12 74; fax 513 12 74-15. 22 rooms. Double 1,100 ÖS. Single 800 ÖS. Breakfast included.
This is in an attractive building in an excellent position.

PENSIONS

These tend to provide modest, family-run accommodation, with limited facilities.

PENSION DR GEISSLER *** **19** O9 U 1, U 4 Schwedenplatz
1, Postgasse 14; tel. 533 28 03; telex 136513; fax 533 26 35. Double 750–1,080 ÖS. Single 740 ÖS. Breakfast included.
Clean, pleasant and in the First District, but no lift.

PENSION NEUER MARKT **** **19** N9 U 1, U 3 Stephansplatz
1, Seilergasse 9; tel. 512 23 16, telex 116890, Fax 513 91 05. 37 rooms. Double 1,320 ÖS. No single rooms. Breakfast included.
This pleasant pension is in a beautiful white stucco building, at the head of a lovely and perfectly located square.

PENSION PERTSCHY **** **19** N9 U 1, U 3 Stephansplatz
1, Habsburgergasse 5; tel. 534 49; fax 53 37 096. 120 rooms. Double 1,140–1,280 ÖS. Single 740 Ö. Breakfast included.*
Highly recommended.

124

PENSION RESIDENZ *** **18** M10 U 2 Schottentor
1, Ebendorferstraße 10; tel. 43 47 86-0; telex 131903; fax 43 47 86-50. 13 rooms. Double 960 ÖS. Single 650 ÖS. Breakfast included.
This is in an excellent position tucked in between the Rathaus (town hall) and the Ringstraße university buildings. It is in the centre and near many tram and U-Bahn routes.

SAISON-HOTELS

These seasonal hotels are available only during the student summer holidays (normally July to September); for the rest of the year they are university hostels.

ACADEMIA ** **18** L9 Tram J, 46 Strozzigasse
8, Pfeilgasse 3a; tel. 42 25 34; telex 114832; fax 42 63 97. 368 rooms. Double 850 ÖS. Single 660 ÖS. Breakfast included.
A huge student hostel in a fun area, a short tram ride from the First District.

AQUILA ** **18** L9 Tram J, 46 Strozzigasse
8, Pfeilgasse 1a; tel. 42 52 35; telex 114832; fax 42 63 97. 74 rooms. Double 660 ÖS. Single 500 ÖS. Breakfast included.
Next door to the Academia, a short tram ride from the central First District.

ATLAS *** **18** L9 U 2 Lerchenfelder Straße
7, Lerchenfelder 1–3; tel. 93 45 48; telex 114832; fax 42 63 97. 182 rooms. Double 960 ÖS. Single 730 ÖS. Breakfast included.
In an interesting part of Vienna and near the First District too.

AVIS ** **18** L9 Tram J, 46 Strozzigasse
8, Pfeilgasse 4; tel. 42 63 74; telex 114832; fax 42 63 97. 72 rooms. Double 740 ÖS. Single 530 ÖS. Breakfast included.
Just opposite the Academia and the Aquila above, a short tram ride from the First District.

HAUS DÖBLING ** **12** L12/13 U 6 Währingerstraße/Volksoper
19, Gymnasiumstraße 85; tel. 34 76 31; telex 132008; fax 32 76 31-25. 560 beds. Double 580 ÖS. Single 340 ÖS. Breakfast included.
A big 1970s block in the Cottage district, halfway between Grinzing and the First District.

125

H aving small children around when you are trying to see the sights can be a traumatic experience. But in Vienna there are many activities for all the family, some more obvious than others. This chapter gives information about activities and shops that are particularly suitable for children. And if it all becomes too much, wherever you are in Vienna you are never far from a park, a duckpond or a playground where children can run around and play.

OUTDOORS

FIAKER RIDE

Why not take the opportunity to see many of the sights of the First District by going for a ride in one of the horse-drawn landaus (*Fiaker*)? It will be a hit with the children and if you don't understand what the Fiaker driver is saying, this book will help you to spot the sights. The places from which such tours depart vary from year to year, but you can always rely on the Heldenplatz and the north side of the Stephansdom.

Parks and Playgrounds

Most of the parks listed under Leafy Retreats have playground facilities but the following are particularly good:

Donauinsel (see page 141). Playgrounds, paddling, skating, etc.

Donaupark (see page 142) Every child will enjoy going up the Donauturm (Danube Tower) in the Donaupark and looking over the surrounding city, river and countryside from its observation platform or cafés.

Pötzleinsdorfer Park (see page 143). Playground, children's zoo.

Prater (see page 143). A delight for children. Wurstelprater, Riesenrad (Giant Ferris Wheel) and Lilliputbahn, small zoo and playgrounds.

Stadtpark (see page 143). Paddling pool for summer, with water-spraying elephants and a chute.

Türkenschanzpark (see page 144). One of the best children's playgrounds in Vienna.

The Old Danube, a paradise for children (and adults).

SWIMMING

There are swimming pools virtually everywhere in the city: a selection of the outdoor pools are listed below, together with any additional facilities offered (including whether there is an indoor pool at the same site).

Pools run by the City of Vienna

Open beginning of May to mid-September, Monday to Friday 9 a.m.–8 p.m., Saturday, Sunday and holidays 8 a.m.–8 p.m. (They close at 7 p.m. at the beginning and the end of the season.) Children under 6 years old free; 6–15-year-olds free Wednesday and Sunday during the summer holidays.

DÖBLINGER BAD   6 M14 — Tram 37 Geweygasse
19, Geweygasse 6; tel. 37 22 18, 37 22 19.
Superb view of Vienna, indoor pool with sauna, heated water, fun pool, chute, children's pool, three children's play areas, shop, restaurant.

HIETZINGER BAD   22 G5 — Tram 62 Atzgersdorfer Straße
13, Atzgersdorfer Straße 14; tel. 804 53 19, 804 53 10.
Indoor pool with sauna, heated water, area for games, restaurant.

KONGRESSBAD   10 H11 — S 45 Hernals
16, Julius-Meinl-Gasse 7a; tel. 46 11 63.
Heated water, fun pool with chute, children's pool, mother and child area, tennis, restaurant.

KRAPFENWALDLBAD — 38A Cobenzlgasse
19, Krapfenwaldgasse 65-73; tel. 32 15 01.
Superb view of Vienna, heated water, children's play area, area for ball games, restaurant.

128 **LAAERBERG BAD** — Tram 67 Altes Landgut
10, Ludwig-von-Höhnel-Gasse 2; tel. 68 23 35.
Heated pools, wave-maker, chute, diving area, water games and other sports facilities, mother and child area, restaurant and other snack bars.

SCHAFBERGBAD   4 G13 — 42B Schafbergbad
18, Josef-Redl-Gasse 2; tel. 47 15 93.

Superb view of Vienna, heated water, diving area, mother and child area, area for ball games, restaurant.

SIMMERING BAD

Tram 71, 72 Weißenböckstraße

11, Florian-Hedorfer-Straße 5; tel. 76 25 68, 76 25 69.

Indoor pool plus sauna, outdoor fun pool including wave-maker, chute, children's pool, area for ball games, restaurant.

STRANDBAD ALTE DONAU   9 R13

U 1 Alte Donau

22, Arbeiterstrandbadstraße 91; tel. 23 53 64.

Delightful setting, bathing beach on 'old' Danube, three pools with heated water, area for games, restaurant.

STRANDBAD GÄNSEHÄUFEL 15 S12

U 1 Kaisermühlen/Vienna
International Centre

22, Moissigasse 21; tel. 23 53 92.

Bathing beach, naturist bathing, pool with heated water, chute, mother and child area, area for ball games, Iceland sauna. Some facilities for disabled people.

Private Pools

THERESIEN BAD   23 J6

U 4 Meidlinger Hauptstraße

11, Hufelandgasse 3; tel. 83 44 35, 83 43 62. Longer opening times on Thursday to 8.30 p.m. and on Friday to 9.30 p.m.

Indoor pool with sauna, heated water, children's play area.

BUNDESBAD SCHÖNBRUNN   22 H6

U 4 Schönbrunn

13, Schönbrunner Schloßpark; tel. 83 01 32. May to September, Monday to Friday 9 a.m.–7 p.m., Saturday, Sunday and holidays 8 a.m.–7 p.m.

Heated water, restaurant.

129

BUNDESSPORTBAD ALTE DONAU   9 R13

U 1 Alte Donau

22, Arbeiterstrandbadstraße 93; tel. 23 53 02, 23 61 13. May to September, Monday to Friday 9 a.m.–7 p.m., Saturday, Sunday and holidays 8 a.m.–7 p.m.

Bathing beach, area for football, restaurant.

STADIONBAD **21** S8/9   🚃 80B Stadionbad
2, Prater, Krieau; tel. 26 21 02, 26 21 04. May, June, September, Monday to Friday 9 a.m.–7 p.m.; July and August, Monday to Friday 9 a.m.–8 p.m. Saturday, Sunday and holidays 8 a.m.–7 p.m. throughout the summer.
Wave-maker, fun pool, chute, children's pool, water-polo pool, diving area, 'Robinson' adventure playground, Punch and Judy show (*Kasperltheater*), tennis, shops, restaurant.

THERMALBAD OBERLAA   Tram 67 Kurzentrum Oberlaa
10, Kurbadstraße 14; tel. 68 16 11-249. Monday 9 a.m.–9 p.m., Tuesday to Friday 9 a.m.–10 p.m., Saturday 9 a.m.–9 p.m., Sunday 8 a.m.–10 p.m., holidays 8 a.m.–6 p.m.
Indoor pool with whirlpool, sauna (also hairdresser and chiropodist), outdoor pool with thermal water, Kneipp pavilion, children's pool, restaurant.

SKATING

In winter, skating is one of the most popular sports for children. There are skating rinks (usually outdoor) scattered all over the city, but by far the most fun is when the Danube freezes and one can skate there, either from the Donauinsel (Danube island) or else in a more organized way on the Alte Donau. If it is cold enough, some of the parks spray water on to the concrete ball-game areas to create an artificial rink.

BOOTSVERLEIH KUKLA **15** S13   U 1 Alte Donau
21, Wagramerstraße 48d; tel. 23 22 33. Weekends only.

BOOTSVERLEIH SCHNEIDER **15** S13   U 1 Alte Donau
21, Wagramerstraße 48b; tel. 23 67 82. Wednesday to Sunday.

DONAUPARKHALLE **14/15** R12   U 1 Kaisermühlen/
Vienna International Centre
22, Wagramerstraße 1; tel. 23 61 23. Mid-September to end of March. Saturday 1–5 p.m., Sunday 8–10.30 a.m., 11.45 a.m.–1.45 p.m., 2.30–5 p.m.

130

EISRING SÜD   Tram 65 Windtenstraße
10, Windtenstraße 2; tel. 64 44 43. Mid-October to end of March. Monday, Tuesday, Thursday, Sunday 9 a.m.–8 p.m., Saturday 9 a.m.–9 p.m., Wednesday and Friday 9 a.m.–10 p.m.
Disco on ice every Friday evening.

WIENER EISLAUFVEREIN **19** N8 Tram D, 71 Lothringerstraße
*3, Lothringerstraße 3; tel. 713 63 53. September to March. Monday,
Tuesday, Thursday to Saturday 9 a.m.–9 p.m., Wednesday 9 a.m.–10
p.m., Sunday and holidays 9 a.m.–8 p.m.*

WIENER STADTHALLE/HALLE C **17** J8 U 6 Burggasse/Stadthalle
*15, Vogelweidplatz 14; tel. 981 00-0. Monday to Friday 1.30–5 p.m.
Saturday, Sunday and holidays 8 a.m.–12 noon and 1–5 p.m.*

SKIING

Most people will enjoy a day outside Vienna skiing in the resorts of Lower
Austria, but there are a few places in the Vienna Woods with small lifts
for (mainly) children to enjoy skiing. They will need their own equipment.

HIMMELHOFWIESE 🚌 53B Innocentiagasse
*13, Am Himmelhof. Information from the lift at the Hohen-Wand-Wiese;
tel. 97 11 57. Ski-lift Monday to Friday 12 noon–dusk, Saturday, Sunday
and holidays 10 a.m.–dusk.*

HOHEN-WAND-WIESE 🚌 249, 449 Hohen-Wand-Wiese
14, Mauerbachstraße 174; tel. 97 11 57. Daily 10 a.m.–10 p.m.
Floodlit piste with the longest ski-lift in Vienna.

SCHI- UND RODELWIESE Tram 67 Altes Landgut
AUF DEN HEUBERGSTÄTTEN
10, near to the Per Albin Hansson Siedlung (housing estate).

CLOTHES

There are many delightful children's clothes shops scattered throughout Vienna; we list only a few. Sizes in Austria are given in the following
form: size 56 cm (newborn), 62, 68 cm (6 months), 74 cm (9 months),
80 cm (12 months), 86 cm (18 months), 92 cm (2 years) and so on. **131**

ASCHENBRENNER **19** N9 U 1, U 3 Stephansplatz
*1, Seilergasse 1; tel. 512 44 02. Monday to Friday 9 a.m.–6 p.m.,
Saturday 9 a.m.–1 p.m.*
A good mixture of children's clothes, some classic, others fashionable,
at staggeringly high prices.

BIMBA 19 N9   U 1, U 3 Stephansplatz
1, Bräunerstraße 10; tel. 533 50 31. Monday to Friday 9.30 a.m.–6 p.m., Saturday 9.30 a.m.–12.30 p.m.
Children's fashion and shoes.

CAJA 19 N9   U 1, U 3 Stephansplatz
1, Wildpretmarkt 8–10, and two other branches; tel. 535 69 22. Monday to Friday 10 a.m.–6 p.m., Thursday 10 a.m.–8 p.m., Saturday 9.30 a.m.–12.30 p.m.
Tempting children's fashions as well as maternity clothes.

MINI HAUS 20 P9/Q8   U 3, U 4 Landstraße/Wien Mitte
3, Galerie, Landstraßer Hauptstraße 98-101, and branches; tel. 712 04 38 . Monday to Friday 9 a.m.–6 p.m., except Thursday 9 a.m.–8 p.m., Saturday 9 a.m.–1 p.m.
Reasonably priced children's clothes.

MOTHERCARE 18 M8   U 2 Mariahilferstraße
7, Mariahilfer Straße 20; tel. 93 01 17.
The Vienna branch of the reliable British chain offering everything from prenatal and maternity equipment to clothes for 5-year-olds.

PRENATAL 19 N9   U 1, U 3 Stephansplatz
1, Goldschmiedgasse 10 (off Stephansplatz) and branches; tel. 535 06 43.
The Italian chain selling all the very latest for children.

SCHWEIGER 19 N9/10   U 1, U 3 Stephansplatz
1, Tuchlauben 13; tel. 533 65 16. Also 8, Alser Straße 45; tel. 43 34 18.
Conventional and formal children's clothes for 0–16-year-olds. Many kilts and sailor suits in evidence.

TOM & JERRY 11 J12   S 45 Gersthof
18, Gersthofer Straße 26; tel. 470 93 70. Monday to Friday 9 a.m.–1 p.m. and 2–6 p.m., Saturday 9 a.m.–12 noon.
Some lovely colourful children clothes, many of them from 'Oilily'.

132

WUZIFANT 20 P8/Q7   U 3, U 4 Landstraße/Wien Mitte
3, Landstraßer Hauptstraße 135; tel. 713 76 44.
Some very colourful and practical children's fashions from Italy, France and Holland, for ages 0–16. They also have plenty of toys and a triple slide to amuse the younger shopper.

SHOES

A good selection of shoes is available from a variety of shops. Only specialist shops tend to have staff trained to fit shoes.

DALDOSCH   11 J12   S 45 Gersthof
18, Gentzgasse 135–7; tel. 479 34 45. Monday to Friday 8.30 a.m.–6 p.m., Saturday 9 a.m.–12.30 p.m.
An excellent range of children's shoes – the well-known and reliable Elefanten and the British favourite Clarks, among others. The helpful staff are trained to fit shoes. They also specialize in orthopaedic shoes.

SCHUHHAUS ZUR OPER   19 N9   U 1, U 3 Stephansplatz
1, Tegetthofstraße 5; tel. 512 47 79. Monday 1–6 p.m., Tuesday to Friday 9 a.m.–12 noon and 1–6 p.m., Saturday 9 a.m.–12 noon.
Children's shoes including Elefanten and Clarks. If requested they will measure the width of the child's foot and can provide shoes in three width fittings.

TOYS

This is a selection of toy shops spread over the various districts in Vienna.

BA BA PO – BANNERT   9 S13   U 1 Kagran
22, Wagramer Straße 56; tel. 23 55 89. Monday to Friday 8.30 a.m.–6 p.m., Saturday 8.30 a.m.–12 noon.
A child's dream, three floors dedicated entirely to toys.

HILPERT SPIELWAREN   9 N9   U 1, U 3 Stephansplatz
1, Schulerstraße 1–3; tel. 512 33 69. Monday to Friday 9 a.m.–6 p.m., Saturday 9 a.m.–12.30 p.m.
A special line in model trains.

KLEINBAHN   18/19 M/N10   Tram 1, 2 Börse   **133**
1, Schottenring 17; tel. 34 34 60. Monday to Friday 9 a.m.–6 p.m., Saturday 8 a.m.–12 noon.
Also at 7, Kirchengasse 9; tel. 93 44 28. Monday to Friday 9 a.m.–6 p.m., Saturday 8 a.m.–12 noon.
The local brand of electric train sets in the usual HO scale – very popular in Austria.

KOBER 19 N9   U 1, U 3 Stephansplatz
1, Graben 14; tel. 533 60 18. Monday to Friday 9.15 a.m.–6 p.m., Saturday 9.15 a.m.–12.30 p.m.
Impressively large toy shop on the Graben. A good selection including lots of cuddly toys. Very friendly service.

MATADOR HAUS 18 L8   Tram 52, 58 Neubaugasse
7, Mariahilferstraße 62. Monday to Friday 12 noon–6 p.m., Saturday 9 a.m.–1 p.m; tel. 93 53 56.
Stocks an incredible selection of Matador, a wooden Meccano-type engineering set.

MODELLBAHN WEST 22 H7   Tram 10 Johnstraße
15, Felberstraße/Johnstraße; tel. 985 81 84. Monday to Friday 10 a.m.–6 p.m., Saturday 9 a.m.–12 p.m.
Specializes in model trains, practically all brands, but particularly good on the very small scales. Also sells used spare parts.

SPIELWURM 18 L8   Tram 49 Neubaugasse
7, Westbahnstraße 20; tel. 93 93 56. Monday to Friday 9.30 a.m.–6 p.m., Saturday 9.30 a.m.–12 noon.
An emphasis on educational and wooden toys.

WIENER SPIELZEUGSCHACHTEL 19 N9   U 1, U 3 Stephansplatz
1, Rauhensteingasse 5; tel. 512 44 94. Monday to Friday 9 a.m.–6 p.m., Saturday 9 a.m.–12 noon.
Excellent selection of wooden toys for all ages, in particular some delicate carved and painted wooden carousels, as well as the standard toy selection. Huge variety of board games and well-stocked children's bookshop. Some lovely ideas for small presents too.

BABIES

Disposable nappies (*Höschenwindeln*), creams, shampoos, babyfoods, etc., can be bought at most supermarkets but are cheapest at the *Drogerie* (drugstores), such as DM or BIPA, which have shops all over the city.

134

The quality of formula milk is consistently high in all the many brands available. The formula is usually marked 1, 2 or 3, depending on the age of the baby. For older babies or toddlers there is a good selection of babyfoods, both in jars (recommended are Hipp – made from organically grown fruit and vegetables – and Alete) and as cereals (Milupa and Hipp). Babyfood is also available from Reformhouses and Perlinger shops (see SHOPPING ON PAGE XX).

Baby clothes are available at most children's clothes shops and at the above-mentioned drugstores, where they are reasonably priced, although not always top quality. Other essential accessories for babies can also be purchased at the drugstores or in the children's shops.

BIPA   19 N9   U 1, U 3 Stephansplatz
1, Kärntnerstraße 1; tel. 512 22 10, and about 60 other branches.

DM   19 N9   U 1, U 3 Stephansplatz
Rotenturmstraße 12; tel. 512 39 60, and about 50 other branches.

MUSEUMS

Further information about most of the following museums can be found in the section on museums.

ERSTE WIENER   U 1 Nestroyplatz
KINDERGALERIE LALIBELA   19 O10
2, Zirkusgasse 3; tel. 64 88 025.
The first Viennese gallery for exhibitions for and by children, including work by young foreign artists. The gallery also offers regular courses to encourage fantasy and creativity.

MUSEUM FÜR VÖLKERKUNDE
This is an interesting museum for children, but the curators are not too happy to see (or hear) small children taking advantages of the sticks with the various percussion instruments! Most children will be fascinated by the section dealing with the American Indians.

NATURHISTORISCHES MUSEUM
Super for kids. One of the few museums in Vienna to make a definite attempt to cater for children. The pre-historic dinosaurs are a great attraction.

135

PLANETARIUM   14 P10   U 1 Wien Nord/Praterstern
2, Prater Hauptallee (near the Ferris Wheel); tel. 24 94 32. Tours for children every Sunday at 9.30 a.m.
A wonderful experience for all children – and educational as well!

PUPPEN- UND SPIELZEUGMUSEUM
This is the Doll and Toy Museum.

WIENER TRAMWAY-MUSEUM
A hit with most children (and fathers). At the weekend it is possible to have a trip on one of the old trams.

ZIRKUSMUSEUM
The Circus and Clown Museum will interest children because of its theme.

EATING OUT

Many restaurants or *Gasthäuser* offer children's menus (usually schnitzel or hamburger), with the usual Mickey Mouse or Donald Duck camouflage to tempt the little ones, and most are quite willing to provide half portions. Sadly it is rare to be offered a high chair or to find an indoor play area, although the lack of high chairs is often compensated for by the appropriate number of telephone directories.

A few places have a garden where children can play.

BELLINO
58B Am Rosenhügel
12, Rosenhügelstraße 26; tel. 804 31 38. Daily 11 a.m.–midnight.
Pizzeria with Viennese cuisine as well. Large garden with playground.

GOLDENER HIRSCH   22 F7
U 4 Unter St Veit
14, Cumberlandstraße 50; tel. 894 27 15. Tuesday to Friday 10 a.m.–midnight, Sunday 8 a.m.–3 p.m.
The main attraction here is the bird and pet market that takes place every Sunday morning. In various parts of the garden you can see (and, if you wish, buy) various birds, including ducks, and rabbits.

HÄUSERL AM STOAN   4 F15
No public transport
19, Zierleitengasse 42a (Höhenstraße); tel. 44 13 77. Wednesday to Sunday 11 a.m.–11 p.m.
Romantic restaurant in the Vienna Woods with a garden and play area outside.

HERMESVILLA
60B Lainzer Tor
13, Lainzer Tiergarten. Wednesday to Sunday 9.30 a.m.–7 p.m.
Garden and playground.

Baby-sitting Services
Baby sitting Zentrale. *16, Herbststraße 6-10; tel. 95 11 35. Monday to Friday 8 a.m-3 p.m. U 6 Stadthalle.*
Trained babysitters over the age of 20 are available.
Institute of European Studies. *1, Johannesgasse 7; tel. 512 26 01-0.* U 1, U 3 Stephansplatz.
During term (mid-September till mid-June) students are available as sitters.
Babysittervermittlung des Österreichischen Hoch-schüler-schaft. *9, Liechtensteinstraße 13; tel. 34 65 18-0. Monday to Friday 9 a.m.–1 p.m.* Tram D Fürstengasse.
American International School. *19 Salmannsdorfer Straße*
The school has a list of high-school students interested in baby-sitting jobs (only evenings and weekends, of course).
Österreichischer Akademischer Gästedienst (Austrian Visitor's Service). *4, Mühlgasse 20; tel. 587 35 25. Monday to Friday 8 a.m.–5 p.m.* U 4 Kettenbrückengasse.
A list of Austrian students willing to babysit is available on demand.

HEURIGER ZIMMERMANN (See RESTAURANTS on page 96.)

LINDWURM   🚌 54B, 55B Slatingasse
13, Ghelengasse 44. Daily except Friday 10 a.m.–9 p.m.
Famous for its large schnitzel. Garden surrounded by woods and fields with lovely view of Vienna.

NAPOLEONWALD   🚌 56B Gnedgasse
13, Jauner Straße 5; tel. 88 11 98. Tuesday 4–11 p.m., Wednesday to Saturday 9 a.m.–11 p.m., Sunday 9 a.m.–10 p.m.
Hot food until 10 p.m. Viennese cuisine with barbecue and seasonal specialities. Large garden – ideal for children.

SCHWEIZERHAUS   **14** Q10   Tram N Prater Hauptallee
2, Straße-des-Ersten-Mai 116-117; tel. 218 05 75. Daily 11 a.m.–11 p.m.
Large garden with children's playground.

137

WEBERHÜTTE   S 40 Kahlenbergerdorf
19, Eisernenhandgasse 2. Monday to Wednesday 12 noon–9 p.m.
Quiet old restaurant on the Kahlenberg with a delightful garden and a view of Vienna.

WIENERWALD RESTAURANTS

This City-Council-owned chain of restaurants has nearly 20 outlets in Vienna and provides solid food at constant standards. They really provide facilities for toddlers (play-areas). For example:

1, Annagasse 3; tel. 512 37 66.
1, Bellariastraße 12; tel. 93 72 79.
1, Freyung 6 (Schottenkeller); tel. 533 14 20.

The last of these is a better address than most, not least for its beautiful quiet garden under chestnut trees, where kids can run around without danger from traffic.

PIZZERIAS

There are innumerable pizzerias all over the city. The standard seldom falls below that acceptable to most children and the quality of the parents' life often improves with food provided at the appropriate moment.

SANDWICH BARS

Any butcher, grocery store or supermarket will make up filled rolls for you. The amount of sausage is usually far beyond what most people would expect so it is often worth buying a few extra rolls and re-dividing the filling. *Extrawurst* is a good standard, but *Krakauer* (ham sausage) or *Käsewurst* (sausage with little bits of cheese in it) will delight most children. In most of these places it is traditional for children to be offered a slice of sausage whilst waiting, too. For some unknown reason it is less common for children to eat cheese in Austria, but the selection is large.

In some bakeries you can buy open sandwiches which are more tempting to look at but less filling and less economical. One exception to this rule is:

DURAN   **19** N9   U 1, U 3 Stephansplatz
1, Rotenturmstraße 11; tel. 533 71 15, and branches. Monday to Friday 8 a.m.–6 p.m., Saturday 9 a.m.–12 noon
Wide selection of open sandwiches and filled rolls to take away or to eat there. Cramped seating makes it less than ideal with children, but the food is great to take away for a picnic.

138

SAUSAGE STALLS

All the Viennese enjoy a snack (or meal) at one of the many *Würstelstände* (sausage stalls) scattered around the city. These sell a wide variety of hot sausages served with rolls or bread. Hot dogs are, of course, also served with a liberal helping of ketchup or mustard. One hot tip (literally) is to try the *Leberkässemmel*. This roll filled with a wedge of sausage is extremely filling and warming on the icy cold days of a Viennese winter. Children will love the sausages.

THEATRE

Few theatres in Vienna specialize in productions for children, though many have one children's item in their programme. Exactly what shows and plays are on can be found in the daily papers, at the tourist information office (1, Opernpassage) or at the town hall (1, Reichsratstraße, Rathaus, back foyer). The following theatres do specialize in children's productions, usually in German of course.

MOKI (THEATER FÜR KINDER) 25 N6   Tram 18 Blechturmgasse
4, Blechturmgasse 14; tel. 505 98 06.
Ambitious modern theatre for children.

THEATER   Tram 52, 58,
DER JUGEND 18 L8   🚌 13A Amerlingstraße
7, Neubaugasse 38; tel. 93 74 42-0, 93 25 46-229.
The only theatre catering for younger teenagers.

Austrian Laws
Some Austrian laws may seem strange as they are unknown in other countries, but they are strict in safeguarding children's interests.
Transport
Children under the age of 12 are not allowed to ride in the front seat of a car and should wear seatbelts in the back.
   Children under the age of 15 can use Viennese public transport free on Sundays, holidays and during the long summer holiday (July and August).
Restaurants
Children up to the age of 14 can remain in restaurants, *Heuriger* and other public places until 9 p.m. if accompanied by an adult; children between 14 and 16 until 11 p.m., if accompanied. 16–18-year-olds can stay until 11 p.m.
Public dances, discos, etc.
Children up to the age of 16 are not allowed to attend such functions; 16–18-year-olds may stay until 11 p.m. (later if supervised).

139

Vienna 's parks offer a welcome break from the busy streets, and all are easily accessible by public transport from the city centre.

PARKS AND OPEN SPACES

ALTE DONAU   8/9/15   U 1 Alte Donau
At one time the Danube meandered over a wide area to the north and east of Vienna. As more and more people began to settle outside the city walls, the threat of flooding became acute, so in 1875 a new, straight channel was dug. The former riverbed has been a favourite recreation area of the Viennese ever since and is known as the Alte Donau (Old Danube). Despite the limited size and depth of this stretch of water it offers many traditional pleasures: sailing or rowing, a swim in the pleasantly warm water, or just a cup of coffee on one of the many terraces that overlook it.

BURGGARTEN   8/9 M/N9   Tram 1, 2 Babenbergerstraße
1, Opernring.
Originally the private domain of the Austrian Court, this garden was given to the public in 1918. The impressive building on your left as you enter from the Ring is the National Library; the building at the far end is the Hofburg palmhouse. The Burggarten is a pleasant place on a hot summer's day, with plenty of shade beneath the large trees. There is a statue of Mozart and monuments to Emperor Franz I and Emperor Franz Josef.

DONAUINSEL   7/8/14/15/21   U 1 Donauinsel
Acessible via all the Danube bridges.
Between 1972 and 1987, as part of the flood-control measures, an unsightly and unused flood plain of the Danube was excavated to form a slow-flowing side branch of the river. The excavated material was used to create an artificial island in the Danube, parts of which were densely

141

The Burggarten – an oasis of calm right in the heart of the city.

planted with fast-growing trees and shrubs, and already the island has a woodland feel about it.

It is an extremely popular place: in summer the paths are full of joggers and cyclists, while the winter brings out cross-country skiers and sledge-pulling parents. The New Danube is ideal for swimming, windsurfing and ice-skating, according to the season.

DONAUPARK   U 1 Kaisermühlen/Vienna International Centre
22, Wagramer Straße/ Arbeiterstrandbadstraße/Donauturmstraße.
This 247-acre (100-ha) park beside the modern UNO-City complex was built on a former rubbish dump to house the Vienna International Horticultural Show in 1964. Nowadays, the walkways, gardens and playgrounds have fewer visitors, and the park is recently reduced in size, but it nevertheless offers a welcome break from sightseeing. There is an 827-ft (252-m) tower with a revolving café on top to give the visitor a panoramic view of Vienna. The giant cross in one of the meadows near the tower commemorates Pope John Paul II's visit to Vienna in 1983.

LAINZER TIERGARTEN   🚌 60B Lainzer Tor
13, Hermesstraße.
The Lainzer Tiergarten is 9.7-square-mile (25-km²) walled-in section of the Vienna Woods west of the city. Maria Theresia had the 15-mile (24-km) wall constructed in 1772 to contain the freely roaming wild boar, elk and deer. The whole park contains 50 miles (85 km) of paths and rises to a height of 1,666ft (508m) at Kaltbründl Hill (with observation platform). It is open from Palm Sunday to early November.

A small part of the park nearest to the town and extending up to the Hermesvilla is actually open all year round (except Mondays and Tuesdays) and is very popular with the Viennese at weekends. It has a nature path and a number of enclosures with wild horses, mouflon, fallow deer etc. Cars, bicycles and dogs are not allowed, so it is a very good park for small children, whose needs are also met by several playgrounds. There are rest areas as well as restaurants.

LOBAU   S 80 Lobau
22, Lobau.
The Lobau is a huge area of relative wilderness, where you can walk or cycle, or go for a swim in one of the many small lakes. Like the Alte Donau, the lakes and nature reserve were formed as a direct result of the first regulation of the Danube's flow. Branches of the divided and meandering river were either filled in and used for development or else, as here, left as unspoilt naturual areas for recreation.

PÖTZLEINSDORFER PARK   4 G/H13   Tram 41 Pötzleinsdorf
18, Geymüllergasse.
This park, at the terminus of the 41 tram, will delight any small child, while
for adults there is the additional attraction of many nearby *Heurigen*.
In the meadow area by the entrance are an enormous sandpit, see-saws,
a slide and swings for the very young, and climbing frames and other
more adventurous equipment for older children. Young and old alike will
enjoy the aviary and children's zoo.

The rest of the park is hilly and wooded, and is very pleasant to walk
through. From the top of the Schafberg is an excellent view of Vienna.

PRATER   20/21   U 1 Wien Nord/Praterstern
2, Praterstern/Prater Hauptallee.
Mentioned in medieval documents as woodlands, the Prater was des-
ignated an imperial hunting ground by Emperor Maximilian II in about
1560. It remained the exclusive property of the court until 1766, when
Josef II opened it to the general public. Shortly afterwards cafés and restaurants opened here, and the area nearest the Praterstern later became
the famous 'Wurstelprater', which now boasts a varied mixture of traditional and ultra-modern rides, arcades and games. Near the entrance
to the Wurstelprater is the Riesenrad (Giant Ferris Wheel: see Sights,
page 33) and the Planetarium

However, the Prater is not merely a pleasure park: there are several
kilometres of sprawling woodlands with ponds and clearings. The Hauptallee (Main Avenue), a 2.8-mile (4.5-km) tree-lined boulevard, is the main
(traffic-free) thoroughfare through the park with the Lusthaus
(Pleasure House) at its far end. This building, formerly on the banks of
the Danube, served as the main hunting lodge for the Prater. It was built
in 1782 by Isidor Canevale and is now a café and restaurant.

Apart from all this, the Prater also has the Lilliput railway, Vienna's
biggest sports arena, Vienna's largest trade fair grounds and the
Freudenau racetrack, where horse races are held most weekends between April and November.

SCHÖNBRUNN PARK (See page 25.)

STADTPARK   19 O8/9   U 4 Stadtpark
1, Parkring.
If you travel away from the inner city towards the Third District, you are **143**
almost certain to pass through the Stadtpark. It extends from the Hilton
Hotel towards the Künstlerhaus, and is flanked by the Ringstraße and
the River Wien.

The Stadtpark contains a well-known statue of Johann Strauss the Younger, playing the violin whilst conducting (the traditional way to conduct a dance orchestra), as well as statues of Franz Schubert, Anton Bruckner and Robert Stolz. There is a pleasant pond and a garden café, the Kursalon, which in summer puts on afternoon concerts.

TÜRKENSCHANZPARK 5 J/K12/13   40A Gregor-Mendel-Straße
18, Hasenauerstraße/Gregor-Mendel-Straße.

This park takes its name from a fiercely fought battle with the Turks that took place here in September 1683, during the siege of Vienna.

Although in a built-up residential area and extending over just 32 acres, this park is a delight to visit. It has been extremely well planned (in 1888 and 1910) and meandering paths are flanked by trees, bushes and flower beds. There are cafés, animal pens, ponds, monuments to the Austrian writers Adalbert Stifter and Arthur Schnitzler, and a watchtower, as well as open grassy areas. One of the great attractions is the stretch of open track, between two tunnels, of the *Vorortelinie*–trains whistle through here several times an hour and can be watched from above.

VOLKSGARTEN 18 M8   Tram 1, 2 Bellaria
1, Burgring.

The Volksgarten was created in the gap made in the wall of the Burgbastei by Napoleon's army in 1809. Its symmetrical design is along classical French lines. In the centre of the gardens are two buildings: the Temple of Theseus (built between 1819 and 1823) and the Volksgarten Meierei, a pavilion café open in summer.

UNDERGROUND TOURS

ST MICHAEL'S MUMMIES   U 3 Herrengasse
1, Michaelerplatz.

Well-preserved mummies from the 17th and 18th centuries on view in the crypt of the Michaelerkirche. Tours vary according to the season.

ST STEPHEN'S CATACOMBS   U 1, U 3 Stephansplatz
144 *1, Stephansplatz.*

Guided tours of the catacombs of the Stephansdom start from the meeting point in the nave when the appropriate number of people has assembled.

VIENNA SEWERS (*THE THIRD MAN*) Tram 1, 2 Oper
Meeting point: 1, Philharmonikerstraße, outside the main entrance of Hotel
Sacher. Run by Vienna Guides; tel. 23 51 99, 36 57 033. 1½ hours.
Visit the dramatic location of the famous final scene of Carol Reed's 1948
film *The Third Man*.

TRAM TOUR

OLDTIMER-TRAMWAY
4, Karlsplatz/Otto Wagner-Pavilion; tel. 587 31 86. Saturday 1.30 p.m.,
Sunday and holidays 10 a.m. and 1.30 p.m.
A sightseeing tour of Vienna by vintage tram, taking in, among other
things, the Ringstraße with all its magnificent buildings.

BOAT TOURS

ERSTES WIENER BOOTSTAXI
1, Riverside Bakery/Abgang Salztorbrücke; tel. 63 96 69. Daily from
2 p.m.
Four floating taxis that will each take a maximum of eight people to any
destination on the Danube or Danube Canal, or give you an individu-
ally tailored sightseeing tour of the city. Booking recommended.

SCHIFFSRUNDFAHRTEN DER DDSG
1, Schwedenbrück; tel. 217 50-450. Daily 10.30 a.m., 1, 2.30, 4.40 p.m.
(calling at Hotel Scandic Crown at 11.40 a.m., 2.10, 3.40, 5.40 p.m.).
A long tour of the Danube and Danube Canal.

AIR TOURS

VIENNAIR-POLSTERERJET
Flughafen Wien; tel. 711 10-2077.
This company runs five standard trips from Vienna's airport at Schwechat. **145**
Flights can be organized for groups of four or more; times of departure
are negotiable. They also offer taxi flights in planes for three or six pas-
sengers. Contact them for further details.

AIRPORT

Vienna airport (Flughafen Wien Schwechat) is about 20 km (12 miles) south-east of the city centre off the motorway to Budapest. The journey should not normally take more than half an hour by car.

CITY AIR TERMINAL

The City Air Terminal is below the Hilton Hotel, opposite the Wien Mitte/Landstraße U-Bahn station.

Buses. A regular shuttle bus runs between the airport and the City Air Terminal at 15-minute intervals.

Luggage cannot be checked in at the City Air Terminal but goes free of charge on the shuttle.

Parking. There are plenty of car parks, covered and uncovered, short- and long-term.

Taxis. Fares are a standard 200 ÖS from the centre to the airport, provided there aren't snarl ups on the way and you have booked an airport taxi.

Mazur Airport Service (tel. 604 91 91, 604 22 33) will collect you from your hotel and take you to the airport and accepts advance bookings for collection from the airport.

Trains. There is a regular train service between the airport and Wien Mitte.

CAR HIRE

ARAC EURODOLLAR RENT A CAR   U 4 Stadtpark
1, Schubertring 9; tel. 75 67 17.
Vienna Airport, Arrivals Hall; tel. 71110-2699, and branches.

AVIS CAR HIRE   U 1, U 2, U 4 Karlsplatz
1, Opernring Hof 1; tel. 587 62 41; also Airport Schwechat; tel. 711 10 27 00.

BUDGET RENT-A-CAR   U 3 Landstraße/Wien Mitte
3, City Air Terminal, Landstraßer Hauptstraße 2A; tel. 75 65 65.

DENZEL   U 1, U 2, U 4 Karlsplatz
1, Kärntnerring 14; tel. 505 42 00.

147

HERTZ   U 1, U 2, U 4 Karlsplatz
1, Kärntner Ring 17; tel. 512 86 77.

MIETWAGEN GÖTH   U 1, U 3 Stephansplatz
3, Johannesgasse 28; tel. 713 71 96. Daily 8 a.m.–6 p.m. including holidays.

CLIMATE

Austria has the perfect climate, warm summers and cold winters with plenty of snow, not too much rain but plentiful water. The average summer temperature is 24° C (75° F), but highs can reach 38° C (100° F), and the average winter temperature is 1° C (34° F), but lows can reach –20° C (–5° F), though these extremes do not usually last long. Winter winds can be bitingly cold.

COURTESIES

Austrians are courteous in a traditional manner. They have a tendency to shake hands whenever they meet a friend or acquaintance, and it is not unusual for a woman to have her hand kissed by a man.

CRIME

Although on the increase, crime is negligible by the standards of other capital cities. There are only a few places that should be avoided after dark: Karlsplatz, some of the stations, e.g. Südbahnhof, Prater fairground or park and the surrounding areas of the Second District.

CUSTOMS AND ENTRY REGULATIONS

Passports are required but visas are not necessary for Canadian, UK and US citizens. The one-year visitor's passport available from UK post offices is acceptable.

There are no restrictions on the amount of foreign currency brought into Austria, but no more than 100,000 ÖS may be taken out without special permission.

DISABLED VISITORS

There are some facilities for people in wheelchairs, but these are not consistent. Pavement curbs are often lowered but they still tend to be above the level of the road. Many public places, such as most U-Bahn stations, have lifts.

A special guide to Vienna for the disabled visitor is available free of charge from the Sozialamt der Stadt Wien, Rathaus on the Ringstraße.

DRIVING IN VIENNA

For the visitor a car is probably more of a liability than an asset. Public transport is excellent and pleasant to use.

Traffic regulations. Drive on the right. Speed limits are 130 kph (80 mph) on motorways, 50 kph (30 mph) in built-up areas, 100 kph (60 mph) elsewhere. Traffic approaching a junction from the right has precedence, except on a main road marked with a yellow diamond, when cars from the right give way. Trams almost invariably have right of way. Do not cross solid lines on the road. Seatbelts must be worn, and children under 12 must sit in the back. Cars must carry an accident triangle, a set of spare bulbs and an emergency first-aid kit.

Parking. Parking rules are complex and confusing for the visitor. Police are keen to clamp or tow away offending vehicles and fines seem to vary from 1,000 to 2,000 ÖS plus the cost of a tow. Retrieving your car from the pound is a major hassle; contact the police. Release from the clamp is expensive but more or less efficient; apply to the police.

In places indicated by blue or white lines on the road (Kurzparkzone) a parking voucher, available from a Tabak Trafik (see POST AND TELEPHONE) must be displayed appropriately marked.

Do not park overnight during the winter months in streets with tramlines – these streets have to be kept clear for snowploughs and you will be towed without warning.

Fuel. Most petrol stations are not open 24 hours, though plenty are. Many do not accept credit cards. Antifreeze is already added to the diesel mixture dispensed from the pumps in winter.

Accidents and emergencies. Contact the ÖAMTC (Austrian automobile and touring club) (1, Schubertring 1–3; tel. 71199) or the similar, but smaller, club, the ARBÖ (15, Mariahilfer Straße 180; tel. 123).

149

ELECTRIC CURRENT

Voltage is 220 V, and plugs are the usual European two-pin plugs.

EMBASSIES

Australia: 4, Mattiellistraße 2–4; tel. 512 85 80-0, 512 97 28-0, 512 97 10-0, 512 97 27-0. After hours; tel. 512 73 71-0.
Canada: 1, Dr-Karl-Lueger-Ring 10; tel. 533 36 91.
Ireland: 3, Landstraßer Hauptstraße 2, Hilton Centre, 16 floor (stock); tel. 715 42 46, 715 42 47, 712 52 39.
New Zealand: 1, Lugeck 1; tel. 512 66 36.
South Africa: 19, Sandgasse 33; tel. 32 64 93-0.
United Kingdom: 3, Jauresgasse 12; tel. 713 15 75.
United States of America: 9, Boltzmanngasse 16; tel. 31 55 11.

EMERGENCY NUMBERS

Fire brigade: tel. 122.
Police: tel. 133.
Ambulance: tel. 144.
Emergency doctors: tel. 141.
Helpline in English (Befrienders): tel. 713 33 74.

GUIDES, TOURS AND TRANSLATORS

At some monuments, museums and exhibitions, taped tour commentaries can be hired.

Coach tours are organized by two firms: Cityrama Sightseeing Tours (1, Börsegasse 1; tel. 534 13-0) and Vienna Sightseeing Tours (3, Stelzhammergasse 4/11; tel. 712 46 83-0 and 715 11 42-0).

If you need a translator or interpreter, ask at the Rathaus information office or at your hotel.

HEALTH AND MEDICAL CARE

There are no immunization requirements for entry into Austria.

Britain has a reciprocal arrangement with Austria whereby medical advice and treatment is given on presentation of a British passport. In-patient treatment is virtually free.

MONEY MATTERS

Currency. The unit of currency is the Austrian Schilling, often abbreviated to ÖS, Sch or AS. The Schilling breaks down into 100 Groschen.

Eurocheques are accepted for sums up to 2,500 ÖS,when supported by a Eurocard, and Eurocards are useful for gaining free entry into many museums.

Currency exchange. Banks are normally open from 8 or 8.30 a.m. to 4 p.m., although smaller branches may close at lunchtime or as early as 3 p.m. in the afternoon. On Thursday banks are open until 5.30 p.m.

At weekends money can be exchanged at the airport, main stations, some hotels, certain Tourist Information Offices, the Reisebüro City on Stephansplatz and the 24-hour post offices in Postgasse and Fleischmarkt and at the main railway stations.

Credit cards are relatively little used in Austria. Most shops and petrol stations and many restaurants do not accept them. Hotels generally do, but check first.

USEFUL ADDRESSES

American Express: 1, Kärntner Straße 21–23; tel. 515 40 65. Lost and stolen travellers' cheques; tel. 0660 391. Lost and stolen American Express cards; tel. 512 97 14.

Creditanstalt-Bankverein: 1, Schottengasse 6–8; tel. 531 31-0.

Diner's Club Austria: 4, Rainergasse 1; tel. 501 35-0.

Erste Österreichische Sparkasse: 1, Graben 21; tel. 531 00-0.

Girozentrale: 1, Schubertring 5–7; tel. 711 94-0. 1, Am Hof 2; tel. 531 24-4, and branches.

Raiffeisenbank Wien: 1, Michaelerplatz 3; tel. 531 73-0, and branches.

Zentralsparkasse: 3, Vordere Zollamtstraße 13; tel. 71191-0.

NEWSPAPERS AND MAGAZINES

English-language newspapers are widely available at news-stands all over the city. European editions of the *Herald Tribune* and the *Financial Times* are both printed in Frankfurt, so same-day editions are available. Other English papers are available later during the day of publication, except Sunday papers, which don't arrive until Monday morning.

Cultural events are listed in the local tabloids (*Kurier*, *Krone*) and also the better papers where they also list the foreign-language films.

POST AND TELEPHONE

Post. The main post offices are 1, Fleischmarkt and 1, Postgasse. The counters for letters there are open 24 hours.

Postboxes are yellow and usually wall-mounted. Stamps are available at post offices (opening hours 8 a.m.–12 noon and 2–6 p.m.) and Tabak Trafiken. These are tobacco shops and newsagents which generally fulfil the function of small post offices in Britain; there is usually a post-box outside.

Telephone. Call boxes located all over the city and particularly in U-Bahn stations are generally clean, undamaged and easy to use, with instructions in diagrammatic form. Some accept ordinary coins and others magnetic phone cards (*Wertkarte*), available from post offices and Tabak Trafiken. Telephone calls from call boxes can normally be made using 1 ÖS, 5 ÖS and 10 ÖS coins, but older boxes have a strange button (*Zahlknopf*) which you need to press as soon as the person you are calling answers the phone.

Inquiries Austria: tel. 16 11

Inquiries abroad: tel. 08

Reverse-charge calls can be made from private telephones and from call boxes marked with an R by dialling 09 to get the operator.

You can dial direct overseas using the following codes:

Australia	00 6
Ireland	00 353
Canada	00 1
New Zealand	00 64
South Africa	00 27
UK	00 44
USA	00 1

PUBLIC HOLIDAYS

There are a lot of these in Austria (see below), most of them religious holy days, many of them moveable, so it is easy to get caught either by all the shops and banks being closed or in traffic jams caused by the large numbers of Viennese try to leaving town on such holidays.

1 January (New Year's Day/*Neujahr*)
6 January (Epiphany/*Dreikönigsfest*)
Easter Monday (*Ostermontag*)
Whit Monday (*Pfingstmontag*)
1 May (*Tag der Arbeit*) no trams in the morning
Corpus Christi (*Fronleichnam*) – on a Thursday in May or June
Ascension Day (*Christi Himmelfahrt*) – on a Thursday in May or June
15 August (Assumption of Mary/*Maria Himmelfahrt*)
26 October (National Day/*Staatsfeiertag*)
1 November (All Saints Day/*Allerheiligen*)
15 November (St. Leopold's Day, Vienna's patron saint): banks shut but shops open
8 December (Immaculate Conception of Mary/*Maria Empfängnis*)
24 December(Christmas Eve/*Heilig Abend*) – everything closes early in the afternoon
25 December (Christmas Day/*Christtag*)
26 December (Boxing Day/*Stefanitag*)
31 December (New Year's Eve/*Silvester*) – shops close at lunchtime

PUBLIC TRANSPORT

Vienna is very well equipped with public transport facilities. There are trams and buses, both running at intervals of about 3–10 minutes until around 8 p.m., when they change to 15-minute intervals. There is also an excellent underground system (called U-Bahn, lines marked U); some underground trains run as often as every 3 minutes all day, others have 3–8 minute intervals. Additionally, there is an efficient network of local trains (called S-Bahn, lines marked S), normally running every 15 minutes.

The only problem with this transport system is that it virtually stops between midnight and 5 a.m., but recently eight lines of night buses have been established which run every hour and take in most of Vienna.

Tickets: You can buy tickets from machines on buses and trams, provided you have the necessary change, but these single tickets are com-

153

paratively expensive, and you are better off buying tickets in blocks of 5 or 10 (*Vorverkaufsscheine*) at the Wiener Stadtwerke outlets (at most U-Bahn stations) or at all Tabak Trafiken. All these single tickets are valid for one journey in roughly one direction, even when you change transport. Even better value is the *Umweltstreifenkarte*, which you can use on eight – not necessarily consecutive – days and which then enables you to use all public transport on those days. (Alternatively, two or more people can use the one ticket, as long as they always travel together). All these tickets have to be clipped in a blue ticket machine on the bus or tram or at the entrance to U- and S-Bahn stations.

RAILWAY STATIONS

Bahnhof Wien Mitte: local trains (S-Bahn) to all destinations, including the line to the airport. It is next to the City Air Terminal, the central bus station and the U-Bahn line stations U 3, U 4 Landstraße/Wien Mitte. 3, Landstraßer Hauptstraße.

Franz-Josefs-Bahnhof: for journeys north – Prague and Berlin, for example. 9, Julius Tandler Platz.

Ostbahnhof: for Eastern Europe (Hungary, Rumania, Poland, Russia).

Südbahnhof: for Styria, Carinthia, Yugoslavia and Italy. The Südbahnhof and the Ostbahnhof are within the same building on 10, Wiedner Gürtel.

Westbahnhof: for all journeys west – Upper Austria, Salzburg, Tyrol and all of Western Europe. 15, Neubaugürtel.

TIPPING

It is normal to tip waiters and waitresses, porters, hairdressers, taxi drivers, cloakroom and lavatory attendants. The custom in restaurants is to round up the sum to include the tip which should be about 10% if service was good.

Porters get 10 ÖS per bag, taxi drivers 10%, at the hairdressers both the hairwasher and the cutter get 10–20 ÖS, cloakroom attendants get 10 ÖS and lavatory attendants 2–5 ÖS.

TOURIST INFORMATION OFFICES

For Vienna: 1, Opernpassage and City Hall Information 1, Rathaus, Rathausstraße; tel. 43 89 89.

For Austria: 4, Margaretenstraße 1; tel. 58 72 000.

MAP SECTION

Key

Scale 1 : 18 000 - 1 : 30 000

ℹ️	**Informationsbüro** Information	Bureau de renseignements	(in Bau) ⊟U⊟	**U- Bahn** Underground	Métro
	Bebaute Fläche Built up Area	Terrain bâti	•⊟7	**Buslinie** Bus	Autobus
	Industrie- und Bahngelände Industrial and Railway area	Terrain Industriel et de Chemin de Fer	(82 A)	**Linie verkehrt nur zeitweilig** Restricted service	Service étroite
	Öffentl. Gebäude Public building	Bâtiment public		**Stadtgrenze** Municipal Border	Limite Municipal
	Park Wald Park Forest	Parc Forêt		**Bezirksgrenze** Adm. dist. bdy.	Limite des Districtes
	Sportplatz Sports field	Terrain de sport	✪	**Polizei** Police	Police
	Friedhof Cemetery	Cimetiére	☺	**Postamt** Post Office	Bureau de Poste
	Autobahn Motorway	Autoroute	✚	**Krankenhaus** Hospital	Hôpital
	Bundesstr. National road	Route nationale	🅂	**Schule** School	Ecole
	Hauptstr. Main road	Route principale	✝	**Ev. Kirche** Prot. Church	Eglise Ev.
	Fußgängerzone Pedestrian precinct	Zone piétonne	✝	**Kath. Kirche** Cath. Church	Eglise Cath.
	Eisenbahn Railway	Chemin de Fer	✞	**Sonst. Kirchen** Other Churches	Autres Eglises
	Schnellbahn (S-Bahn) Suburban railway	Train regional	🎭	**Theater** Theatre	Théâtre
	Industrie- u. Güterbahn Freight traffic only	Industr. et de Marchandies	🚕	**Taxistand** Taxi rank	Station de Taxis
•⑤	**Straßenbahn** Tramway	Tramway	⊜	**Hallenbad** Indoor swimming- pool	Piscine
			⊝	**Freibad** Open- air swimming pool	Piscine de plein air

Overall map p. 2: numbers in blue refer to map pages

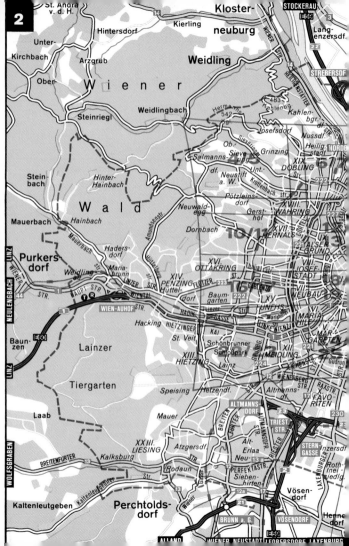

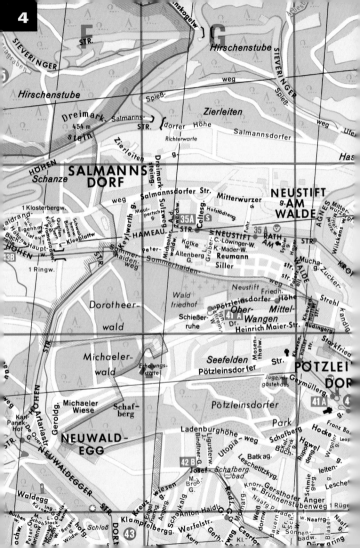

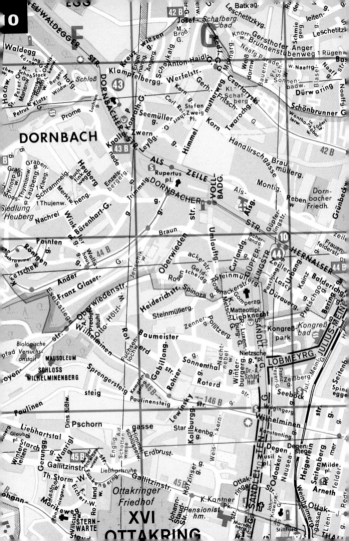

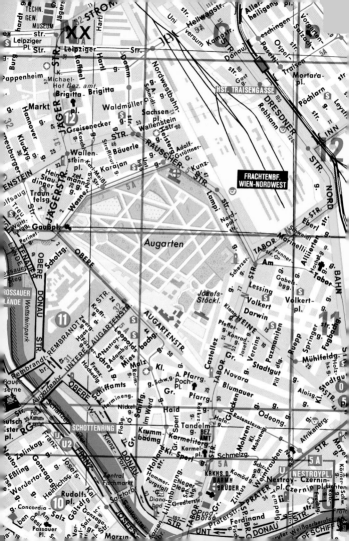

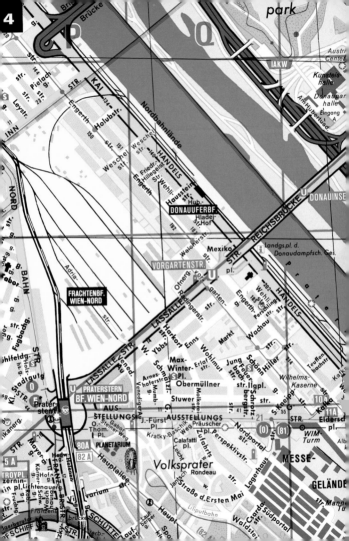

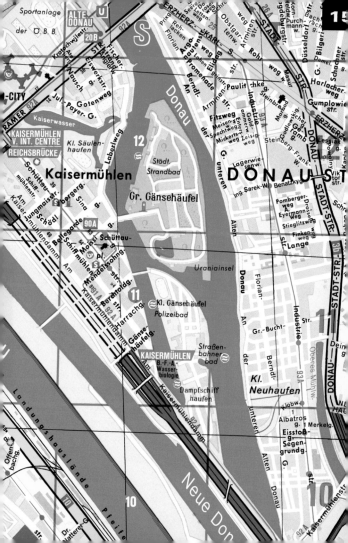

8

Schnell- und Regionalbahnlinie mit Station
Schnellbahnlinie mit Station
Regionalbahnlinie mit Station
U-Bahnlinie mit Station
Lokalbahn Wien-Baden mit Station
Linienbezeichnung Schnellbahn
Linienbezeichnung Regionalbahn
Linienbezeichnung U-Bahn
siehe ÖBB-Fahrpläne

R 10
U1

187

189

191